SpringerBriefs in Computer Science

For further volumes:
http://www.springer.com/series/10028

Benjamin S. Riggan • Wesley E. Snyder
Cliff Wang

Fundamentals of Sketch-Based Passwords

A General Framework

 Springer

Benjamin S. Riggan
Department of Electrical and Computer Engineering
North Carolina State University
Raleigh, North Carolina
USA

Wesley E. Snyder
Department of Electrical and Computer Engineering
North Carolina State University
Raleigh, North Carolina
USA

Cliff Wang
US Army Research Office
Durham, North Carolina
USA

ISSN 2191-5768   ISSN 2191-5776 (electronic)
SpringerBriefs in Computer Science
ISBN 978-3-319-13628-8   ISBN 978-3-319-13629-5 (eBook)
DOI 10.1007/978-3-319-13629-5

Library of Congress Control Number: 2014957406

Springer Heidelberg New York Dordrecht London

Printed on acid-free paper

Springer is part of Springer Science+Business Media (www.springer.com)

This book is dedicated to my beloved wife, Alyssa, who has always supported me in all my endeavors.

Preface

The purpose of this book is to introduce the fundamental procedures necessary for implementing a "sketch-based authentication system." The notion of using a drawing or sketch originally came from Xiaogang Wang, who thought random alphanumeric strings were too complicated to remember. This idea combined with biometric information (e.g. pressure, velocity, or acceleration) posed an interesting, yet difficult problem to solve.

This book is intended for researchers interested in pattern recognition applications similar to the application of sketch-based passwords, such as signature recognition methods, graphical passwords, biometrics, or human-computer interaction techniques. First, concepts utilized by other alternatives to traditional passwords are introduced and analyzed, Then, two different pattern recognition techniques that may be used for recognizing sketch-based passwords (including any associated biometric information) are discussed in detail. Lastly, fundamental theory and experiments related to the security and usability of sketch-based passwords are provided.

Thanks to Wesley E. Synder and Xiaogang Wang for their contributions to this work, without whom this would not have been possible.

Raleigh, NC   Benjamin Riggan

October 2014

Acknowledgements

The information presented in this book is based on work funded by the United States Army Research Office (ARO) grant W911NF-04-D-0003-0019.

Contents

Chapter 1
Introduction

Abstract Keeping data, which is stored on a variety of information systems, e.g. networks, desktop and laptop computers, personal digital assistants (PDAs), smartphones, tablets, or any other electronic media, private is essential for individual security, corporate security, and national security. While a majority of authentication mechanisms remain the same as they were more than a decade ago, attacks on information system infrastructures are becoming more sophisticated. Many, including financial institution, government agencies, and large organization, have always invested both time and money into improved security solutions. One emerging topic, namely sketch-based passwords, is the subject of this brief. In this chapter, the need for alternative security solutions is greatly emphasized, and the fundamental concept of using sketch-based passwords (one possible solution) is introduced. Additionally, the major contributions and results presented in this brief are summarized.

Keywords Privacy · Security · Sketch-based passwords · Authentication

The privacy of critical information, such as credit card numbers, social security numbers, usernames/passwords, and etc., is a huge problem for individuals, businesses (small and large), and governments. The world has become more connected, computers have become faster, and hackers more sophisticated, yet the majority of systems still rely on traditional passwords and encryption mechanisms to provide security of such information.

Passwords are not the only way to protect private information. Authentication systems are based on one or more of the following queries: *what a users carries* (e.g. identification cards), *what a user knows* (e.g. passwords or personal identification numbers), or *who a users is* (e.g. fingerprint or facial recognition). Authentication systems based on each query have respective strengths and weaknesses. Identification (ID) cards and electronic keys provide a simple and easy to use security solution which are effortless to maintain (i.e. revoke, alter, and issue), but they are also relatively easy for unauthorized personnel to steal and duplicate. Passwords are also fairly effortless to maintain, but if passwords do not adhere to certain requirements:

- be 10–15 characters long
- contain both upper and lowercase letters
- contain numbers (0–9)
- contain special characters (e.g. *!, , #, $, %, &. , (, or)*)
- not contain dictionary words

© The Author(s) 2014
B. S. Riggan et al., *Fundamentals of Sketch-Based Passwords*,
SpringerBriefs in Computer Science, DOI 10.1007/978-3-319-13629-5_1

then security may be compromised. Biometrics systems are thought to be the most secure type of authentication system, however, they too have their drawbacks, including: reliability and template security issues.

In general, there are at least two types of users: those that knowingly disregard security measures and those that breach security while adhering to the protocols listed above. Typically, users of the first type use simple and insecure passwords for all authentication systems because the passwords are often convenient and easy to remember. The consequence of this *usability*, of course, is poor *security*. The second class of users create sufficiently complex passwords, however, they usually breach security by writing down usernames/passwords or saving them in a unencrypted file called "passwords" (and more importantly these passwords do not change). The goal of this work is to study the tradeoff between convenience and security using an alternative authentication method, namely sketch-based passwords.

1.1 Sketch-Based Passwords

In this brief, various approaches are considered for recognizing sketch-based passwords. In general, a sketch (or drawing) is used as the means of authentication. The information used (e.g. spatial, temporal, or biometric) for matching sketches may vary depending the approach or hardware used. Usually, sketch-based authentication systems are *online*, meaning sketches are capturesd using a digitizer, tablet computer, or any other device capable of measuring drawing information directly. On the contrary, *offline* systems use a camera, scanner, or other device to take a snap shot of the final drawing. Although recognition of sketches is possible with an offline system, here, only online systems are discussed.

There are many advantages of sketch-based passwords, including:

- easy to remember
- secure
- cost efficient
- robust

A sketch, opposed to a random alphanumeric string, is easier remember because most people prefer shapes and visual patterns over random character strings. Additionally, modern handwriting and pattern recognition algorithms offer excellent performance when it comes to security. Plus, the addition of biometric information to the spatial content of the drawing provides even better security. The ubiquitousness of tablets and other digitizers makes these systems more affordable and keeps development costs to a minimum. A sketch-based password also has the advantage over existing authentication systems because a sketch may combine multiple queries in to one system: what a user knows (i.e. the sketch) and who a user is (i.e. the biometrics). Thus, a sketch-based authentication system may be more robust than authentication systems base on a single query.

Sketch-based passwords do not come without difficulties. Since this type of system requires the interaction between a user and computer, the human-computer interaction (HCI) process complicates the analysis. There are a few fundamental questions that this brief attempts to address (to a certain degree):

1. How well can a user replicate his/her own sketch-based password?
2. How secure are such sketch-based authentication systems compared to similar systems?
3. Compared to other types of systems?

The philosophy of a sketch-based authentication system may be considered similar to online or offline signature recognition. However, let it be stated clearly that in this text, the application is more general than recognition of signatures alone. In most cases, the assumption is that a user will choose a sketch that is less complex[1] than a signature. However, signatures or pseudo-signatures are certainly viable "passwords."

1.2   Contributions

The main contribution of this brief is the analysis of sketch-based passwords *with biometric information*, which specifically includes the testing of the generalizable framework for recognition. Using this framework, additional theory is provided in the application of sketch-based passwords, including: computational complexity and the security/usability tradeoff. Additionally, we demonstrate that sketch-based passwords are an effective means for authenticating users by performing experiments with both synthetic and hand-drawn datasets, including two different hand-drawn datasets (collected using separate devices and/or technologies). One biometric, namely pressure, is successfully shown to improve performance when jointly modeled with sketch-based passwords. Lastly, the HCI process is studied for sketch-based passwords.

1.3   Primary Results

The major results presented in the latter chapters of this work are the following:

1. 0.0 % equal error rate (EER) on a set of synthetic shapes
2. 1.4 % EER (random forgeries) and 28.0 % EER (skilled forgeries) on "doodles" or sketches from the DooDB database [1] *without biometrics*
3. 1.6 % EER (random forgeries) and 23.3 % EER (skilled forgeries) on pseudo-signatures from the DooDB database [1] *without biometrics*

---

[1] Complexity may be considered as the number of self intersection or the number inflection points of curvature.

4. 0.0 % EER (random forgeries) and 3.3 % EER (skilled forgeries) on a set of hand drawn sketches (using four exemplars to construct a representative model)
5. 1.74 % EER (random forgeries) and 16.75 % EER (skilled forgeries) on the BioSketch database [2]

The terms *random* and *skilled* forgeries will be discussed in detail in Sect. 2.1.

These results demonstrate the effectiveness of the approach on a variety of datasets, multiple users (genuine and forgers), and under many conditions. Refer to the main text for complete details regarding each experiment.

1.4   Organization

This remaining chapters in this book are organized as follows:

Chapter 2 introduces graphical passwords and biometric systems. These topics provide the necessary background information for developing a sketch-based authentication system. This is chapter provides the essential analysis of existing frameworks, so that researchers and developers alike may learn and understand the tradeoffs associated with these systems.

Next, approaches to sketch-based authentication are discussed (Chap. 3), including: a dynamic time warping (DTW) approach and a generalized Simple K-Space (SKS) approach. This chapter introduces these algorithm, specifically, in the context of recognizing sketch-based passwords.

Chapter 4 discusses the security and usability tradeoff for sketch-based passwords. Here, the controllability of this tradeoff with algorithm parameters is demonstrated (using the SKS approach) by discussing claims/theorems related to uniqueness and robustness.

HCI considerations are discussed in Chap. 5. In this chapter, the fundamentals of performing a variability analysis are discussed. Using multiple similarity/dissimilarity measures, the analysis is provided using a set sketches provided by the "BioSketch" database [2].

Experiments and results are provided in Chap. 6. SKS is compared with the state-of-the-art, and experiments are conducted in order to demonstrate the benefits of incorporating biometric properties with sketch-based passwords.

Lastly, a summary of this work is provided with the resulting implications and conclusions in Chap. 7. Additionally, future work and possible extensions are briefly stated.

References

1. M. Martinez-Diaz, J. Fierrez, and J. Galbally. The DooDB Graphical Password Database: Data Analysis and Benchmark Results. *IEEE Access*, 1:596–605, 2013.
2. B. S. Riggan, W. E. Snyder, X. Wang, and J Feng. A human factors study of graphical passwords using biometrics. *Proc. of the 36th German Conf. on Pattern Recognition*, 2014.

Chapter 2
Background

Abstract The most relevant work related to sketch-based authentication systems is discussed in this chapter. There are three primary areas of focus: terminology, graphical authentication systems, and biometric systems. All the terminology introduced not only occurs within this brief, but throughout the literature. These definitions are introduced first so that the likelihood of misinterpretation is minimal. Graphical authentication mechanisms may be based on global cognitive recognition, local regions of interest, or relatively simple drawings. This brief only focuses on the latter. Biometrics, which may conceivably be considered a completely independent topic, are thought to provide the best possible security. For all intents and purposes, graphical authentication and biometric security are completely separate problems. However, after understanding the intricate details for each problem, the recognition problem associated with graphical passwords fused with biometric information is more easily comprehensible.

Keywords Passwords · Authentication · Security · Graphics · Biometrics

In this chapter, existing graphical password and biometric systems are discussed. Understanding the design tradeoffs for each problem is useful for developing an effective sketch-based authentication system, especially one incorporating biometric information. Mostly, graphical passwords and biometrics are considered independently, but in Chap. 3 frameworks that jointly recognize graphical passwords and biometrics are introduced.

Graphical passwords and biometrics are considered separately because, in general, they are vastly different problems. Each problem has respective benefits and consequences. Understanding these tradeoffs is critical for fusing the usability of a graphical password with the security of biometrics. Considering the problems separately provides a better basis for designing a joint graphical biometric framework.

2.1 Terminology

Before discussing various methods, some terminology must be introduced for better clarity. In general, there are two modes of operation for almost all authentication systems: *enrollment* and *login*. Enrollment is, typically, when a user initially registers into the authentication system as an authorized user, and login is where a user

© The Author(s) 2014
B. S. Riggan et al., *Fundamentals of Sketch-Based Passwords*,
SpringerBriefs in Computer Science, DOI 10.1007/978-3-319-13629-5_2

attempts to gain access by verifying that he/she is approved to access the information system. Determining the authentication status of a user varies depending on the type of system (e.g. text-based, token-based, or biometric-based). For example, text-based passwords rely on a simple string comparison; token-based grant access purely based on validity of the token (e.g. key or ID card); and biometrics rely on complex recognition algorithms.

There are also some terms that are used, sometimes interchangeably, which apply specifically to biometric systems. Among pattern recognition literature, the terms *recognition, matching, identification,* or *verification* may be confused or even used in place of each other. However, these terms have contrasting definitions. *Recognition* is a rather convoluted word, which implies the autonomous detection of something, e.g. face recognition means the detection of faces. Sometimes, recognition is used in place of matching, identification, or verification. The keyword: *matching* implies the process of determining whether two or more items exhibit some type of similarity (or correspondence). For example, the goal of this text is to determine if one sketch-based password matches another. *Identification* and *verification* are terms corresponding to specific sub-problems often found in pattern classification applications (signatures, sketch-based passwords, or other patterns). The identification problem attempts to determine the correct user using similarity values between a particular instance of a pattern and templates stored with every user in a database. Whereas, the verification problem compares an instance with the template of one particular user. Note the subtle difference: identification makes multiple comparisons, and verification only performs one.

There is also some specific terminology used in regards to the performance analysis of both authentication and biometric systems. In general, there are two types of users: *genuine users* and *forgers* (see Remark 2.1). Genuine users are the ones that should be allowed access, and forgers are those that should be denied.

Remark 2.1 There are many types of forgeries, and thus different types of forgers. Brute force forgeries are essentially "unskilled" random guesses; Shoulder surfing forgeries are observation-based "skilled" forgeries; Phishing forgeries are theft-based "skilled" forgeries.

Usually, there are two types of forgeries considered: *random* and *skilled*. A random forgery, as the name suggest, is a random attempt to gain access (e.g. guessing a user's password). A skilled forgery is an intelligent attempt to gain access that is usually based on prior knowledge (e.g. observing all or part of a user's password).

Ideally, the goal is to "accept" (or grant access to) as many genuine users as possible, while "rejecting" as many forgeries as possible. Equivalently, the objective is to simultaneously minimize the percentage of false rejections (of genuine users) and the percentage of false acceptances (of forgers). Therefore, system performances are usually reported in the form of a *false acceptance rate* (FAR) vs. *false rejection rate* (FRR) curve, which is similar to a *receiver operating characteristic* (ROC) curve (used in other pattern recognition applications). This type of analysis is provided in Chap. 6.

2.2   Graphical Passwords

In this section a taxonomy of graphical passwords is provided. Each method may be categorized as one of the following three types (as suggested by [6]):

1. Cognometric systems—approaches based on image recognition
2. Locimetric systems (in [35] called search metric systems)—approaches based on recognition of image interest points (or regions)
3. Drawmetric systems—approaches based on recognition of a drawing or sketch.

2.2.1   Cognometric Systems

The first type of graphical password takes advantage of the power of the human visual system's ability to recognize faces, objects, scenes, and other visual patterns (often found in images). Cognometric graphical passwords assume that cognitive recognition is easier than recalling a text-based password. Therefore, instead of remembering a (possibly) long and complex string of letters, numbers, and special characters, a user is presented with a random set of images; one containing a (hopefully) secret subset of "correct" faces for authentication purposes.

Similar to most authentication systems, there are two phases: enrollment and login. During user enrollment, a user is presented with a random set of images. These images may be faces, objects, or anything other type of image. The user is required to select a subset of the displayed images to be a "password" for verification purposes. Then, at login time, the correct subset of images are display among an assortment of other images. From the set of images, a user is supposed to correctly recognize and indicate the subset of images corresponding to his/her "password."

One example of a cognometric graphical password is PassFaces^{TM} [31]. In this particular, system users are presented a random set of images of individual faces (i.e. one face per image). The user is able to construct a "password" by selecting a subset (or sequence) of the faces as the means for authentication.

In every authentication system the hope is to completely eliminate predictability in order to provide a "perfectly secure" system. However, in practice, it cannot be completely eliminated (only reduced). Consider any template in an authentication database to be an encoding of any "password." In information theory and cryptography, this is called a *ciphertext* [24]. Ideally, the template (or ciphertext) should provide no information about the original "password" (or plaintext). Commonly, perfect security is violated by user choice or preference.

In general, users prefer "usability" over "security" when it comes to authentication systems. Therefore, given a choice users construct simple passwords that are easier to use and remember, but are consequently less secure. Studies [5, 36] have shown that user preference affects PassFaces™ too. Statistically, people tend to exhibit a bias toward particular types of faces, such as faces with certain skin tones, eye colors, face shapes, and so forth.

In order to address the problem of user preference in PassFaces™ and similar systems, Déjà Vu [7] another cognometric approach uses random patterns and artwork to reduce the amount of predictability from user preference.

2.2.2 Locimetric Systems

An alternative to the image recognition approach to graphical passwords is the locimetric approach. Locimetric systems leverage the innate ability for human attention to be drawn to specific locations (or regions) with in a particular image. This class of systems uses a larger image, which usually contains many points of interest (e.g. edges, corners, shapes, colors, textures, etc.), to stimulate a user's memory. Locimetric systems attempt to minimize the amount of information that a user must remember.

In locimetric systems, during enrollment, a user selects an order sequence of locations within one or more large images. Then, at login, the user must select the correct set of locations from the the displayed image(s). Note, if any one location is incorrect or in the wrong order then access is denied because the "password" is the strictly ordered set of locations. This is similar to text-based passwords.

A canonical example of a locimetric system is PassPoints [43–45]. This system provides a user with a "busy" image—one with many interest points. In this particular system, only one image is provided, and the user is supposed to select 5 distinct locations in that image for purposes of authentication.

Cued Click-Points [2, 3] differs from PassPoints by presenting a user with multiple images (one after another). In each image the user selects only one point (or region). After all images have been presented, the ordered sequence of points from the respective images composes the "password."

2.2.3 Drawmetric Systems

Lastly, drawmetric graphical password systems are drawing-based (i.e. sketch-based) authentication techniques. Drawmetric password recognition most closely resembles traditional shape recognition applications (opposed to text-based passwords) due to similar issues with similarity transformations and noise. But, shape is only one component of drawmetric graphical passwords. Drawmetric passwords also incorporate other properties, such as: parameterization, dynamics, and biometrics. This is further discussed in Chap. 3.

The advantages of drawmetric passwords over text-based approaches included improved memorability, usability, and complexity. Potential concerns include aspects of security, such as vulnerability to brute force, spoofing, and man-in-the-middle attacks, and undefined rules for "proper password" synthesis.

A typical drawmetric system requires a user to enroll by providing one or more instances of a drawing or sketch-based password. From the examplar drawing(s), a template is constructed and stored in a database. Then, during login, the user is expected to recall and reproduce the drawing (i.e. the drawing provided during enrollment) with a sufficient level of accuracy.

Draw-A-Secret [22] is one of the most exemplary drawmetric systems. Draw-A-Secret simplifies the matching problem by encoding the drawing into a easily comparable string. This is performed by using a coarse grid to convert the drawing into a string. A number (or letter) is assigned to each of the grid cells as a label; a particular grid label is recorded as part of the encoded string when the drawing enters the corresponding grid cell. This process produces a string, which like text-based passwords, can easily be matched for the purposes of authentication.

The encoding scheme is demonstrated in Fig. 2.1.

There are multiple extensions to the Draw-A-Secret philosophy that attempt to provide additional security and better performance. Some of these extensions include using background images [8], smaller grid cells [12], and adding stroke color [14, 42].

There are at least two fundamental problems with the Draw-A-Secret methodology, which are: limited invariance to similarity transformations (e.g. translation, rotation, and scale) and quantization errors near intersection points of grid cells. In [41], the latter is alleviated by anchoring the drawing to grid intersection points. This approach encodes a sketch using horizontal, vertical, and diagonal segments. Note the similarity between [41] and chain codes. However, the difference is in the former the number of possible *codewords* or characters depends on the number of grid intersection points, whereas the latter construct a string from only 8 codewords corresponding to the 8 possible directed segments.

In Chap. 3, two more sophisticated sketch-based recognition methods are discussed: dynamic time warping (DTW) and Simple K-Space (SKS). However, a necessary review of biometric systems is provided first.

2.3 Biometric Systems

A biometric property is an attribute that may be used to identify an individual (e.g. DNA, fingerprint, face, gait, handwriting, etc.). Figure 2.2 shows example biometrics used in various recognition applications.

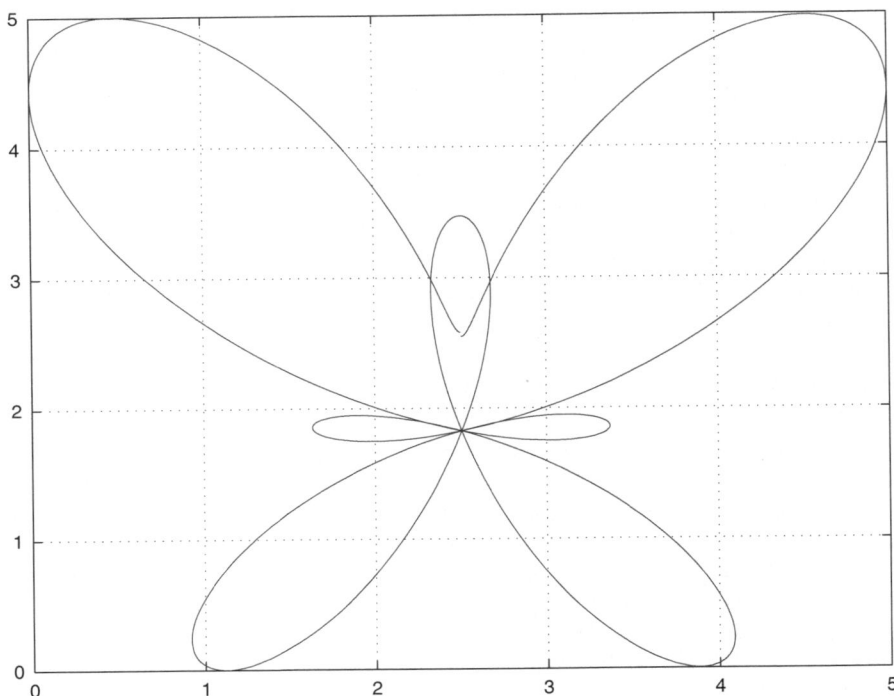

Fig. 2.1 Draw-A-Secret: the coarse grid with is used to encode the drawing. Let the labels, A–Y (first 25 letter of the alphabet), correspond to the cells in raster scan ordering, starting with the grid cell in the upper-leftmost corner. The *butterfly curve* begin in the *center cell* and continues up and to the *right*; it also ends in the *center cell*, coming from the *upper left*. Therefore, the *butterfly curve* corresponds to the following encoding: *MHIDEJONMR-QVUVWR-MHMR-WXYXSR-QR-SR-MLKFABGHM*. Note the *dashes* are only for readability

A biometric system recognizes individual using such biometric properties [10]. Recently, biometrics have become ubiquitous in various technologies, including in commercial/government access systems, personal computers (desktops and laptops), and smart devices (phones and tablets). Biometrics are quickly becoming a key component of security in our society, and they have dramatically increased in popularity.

Ideally, a biometric should, according to [21] possess all of the following qualities:

- universal
- distinct
- permanent
- collectible

Universality means that a biometric must, generally, be useful for identification purposes over sufficiently large population. Distinctness indicates that a certain property

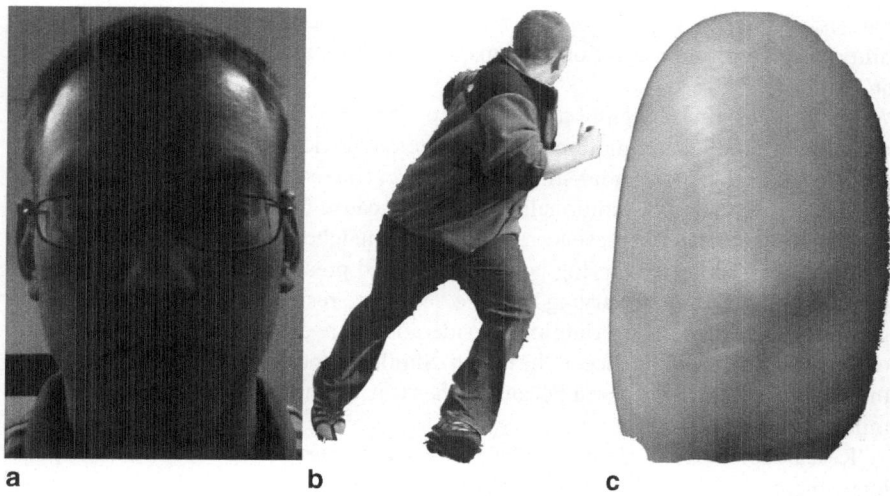

Fig. 2.2 Common biometrics: **a** face, **b** gait, and **c** fingerprints

must be unique to every individual Permanence means that the biometric must not significantly change over time, and collectibility means that the property must be quantifiable.

Remark 2.2 Typically, biometrics do not exhibit *all* properties (at the same time).

For example, some biometrics may be altered or intentionally changed (e.g. gait). In practice, though, a biometric should exhibit more than one of the qualities listed above.

Biometrics are also considered be more secure than traditional authentication mechanisms (i.e. passwords and PINs) because of the aforementioned qualities. However, robust and reliable recognition of most biometrics remains to be a challenging task. Some of these challenges for specific biometrics are discussed.

2.3.1 Fingerprints

One of the most widely accepted biometrics is fingerprints (see [28, 34]). They have been implemented in in the following areas: federal and state government databases, forensic applications, and consumer products. Despite the vast applicability of fingerprint recognition systems, there remain many questions of reliability and security.

Most fingerprint recognition systems are extremely sensitive to various types of noise, such as moisture, motion blur, and internal device noise. Such noise complicates the detection of minutia—distinctive fingerprint feature including ridge endings and ridge bifurcations. Additionally, noise may cause false breaking or bridging of ridges. Therefore, in the presence of noise false matches are easy to encounter.

In addition to noise, varying poses and applied pressures of fingers increase the difficulty of recognition. Varying the pose of fingers, results in partially occluded fingerprints. Occluded fingerprints are considerably more difficult to recognize because of the reduction in confidence of the match. Similarly, the confidence is reduced when the applied pressure is altered because either true minutia may be obscured or false minutia may be produced.

Researchers have made great advances toward overcoming some of these problems, increasing the reliability of fingerprint recognition systems. However, one fact remains: no recognition approach is capable of overcoming a sufficiently poor fingerprint scan[1]. Noise may be reduced (to some degree) and optimization methods can improve performance when fingerprints are partially occluded. However, these approaches have fundamental limitations.

2.3.2 *Faces*

Another well studied class of biometric systems is facial recognition. The human visual system is adept at recognizing faces, which is helpful for identification of individuals. Replicating the recognition rates in digital biometric system, however, is rather difficult for similar reasons discussed in 2.3.1 and more.

Facial recognition approaches encompass a diverse set of solutions, which are not comprehensively discussed here. However, the literature on this subject is extensive (see [47]). Essentially, all facial recognition systems boil down to the detection of facial features (like fingerprints depended on detection of minutia).

There are a multitude of features used: edges [11] and SIFT features [13]. Recently, a lot of work has gone into machine learning approaches that learn a hierarchy of low-to-high level features [40], which pushes the boundaries of recognition performance by learning deep hierarchies of features. Each method is sensitive to noise, occlusion, and pose variations. In different ways, noise, occlusion, and contrasting poses potentially degrade the ability of detecting important features (e.g. eyes, nose, and mouth), thus reducing the recognition performance.

---

[1] This fact is why most governmental fingerprinting is performed by trained professionals, who position and hold fingers during the procedure.

Table 2.1 List of common local features used in handwriting applications

Feature	Description
Time	The total time required to write [15, 23]
Bounding box	The total writing area required [25]
Pen ups	The total number of times a user lifts up the pen (or finger) while writing [15]
Pen downs	The total number of times a user presses the pen (or finger) tip down [15]

2.3.3 Handwriting

Handwriting recognition systems are also perceived as biometric systems because trained experts are able to verify if a handwritten document is a forgery, or if represent the genuine penmanship of a particular person. As with other biometrics, autonomous recognition is convoluted by many factors, including: noise, occlusion, and nonlinear deformation.

Noise, specifically in handwriting applications, is mostly exhibited in the form of jitter. However, in handwriting biometric systems, device noise may exist in the form of sampling errors. Partial occlusions occur when some portion of the either intentionally or haphazardly omitted. Probably one of the most interesting problems in handwriting recognition is determining how to construct representations that are invariant to many nonlinear deformations (especially in the presence of noise and occlusions).

There have been many applications of handwriting recognition, including print or cursive [26, 29], various languages (e.g. Chinese [27, 46], Arabic [16], and Latin [32]), characters [1], or digits/numbers [4], and even context specific handwriting recognition (e.g. dates and checks [18]). Additionally, there have been multiple features used in handwriting recognition, some of which are summarized in Tables 2.1 and 2.2.

2.3.4 Multiple Biometric Systems

Many, including [19, 30, 37, 38] have proposed various methods for fusing multiple biometrics in one unified framework. These system are also advantageous because security is dramatically improved. The tradeoff is, of course, the complications in the recognition of more than one type of biometric. Common issues of such systems include varying descriptor lengths for different biometrics and how/when to combine biometric information (low-level fusion, mid-level fusion, or high-level fusion). While the purpose of this work is not directly related to multi-biometric systems, they are worth noting because according to [39] fusing biometrics at the feature level (i.e. low-level) offers better performance than fusion at the score or decision levels (i.e. high-level).

Table 2.2 List of common global features used in handwriting applications

Feature	Description
Position	The x and y coordinates of each sample point, typically with respect to some reference [33]
Displacement	The difference in x, Δx, and the difference in y, Δy, between sample points [20, 25]
Velocity	The instantaneous rate of change in position with respect to time [23, 33]
Acceleration	The instantaneous rate of change in velocity [17, 23, 33]
Pressure	The point-wise amount of force applied at the pen (or finger) tip by the user in the process of writing [9, 17, 33]
Curvature	The point-wise measure describing the amount of deviation from a line, which is commonly used to model shape [20]
Azimuth	The angle between the pen's projection on the table and the tablet's coordinate reference angle [9]
Altitude	The angle between the pen and the tablet [9]

2.4   Key Points

The main observations to remember from this chapter include:

1. There many types of forgeries, but they are usually classified as "random" or "skilled."
2. There are three common graphical passwords: cognometric, locimetric, and drawmetric.
3. Drawmetric graphical passwords are sketch-based approaches.
4. Advantages of drawmetric systems include: improved memorability, usability, and password complexity.
5. A major disadvantage is that a more complicated matching algorithm is required.
6. Biometrics possess one or more of the following properties: universality, uniqueness, permanence, and collectibility.
7. Handwriting biometric may fused directly into a sketch-based authentication framework.

References

1. M. I. Bernstein. Computer recognition of on-line, hand-written characters. Memorandum RM-3753-ARPA, The RAND Corporation, Santa Monica, California, October 1964.
2. S. Chiasson, P. C. Van Oorschot, and R. Biddle. Graphical password authentication using cued click points. *12th European Symposium on Research in Computer Society*, pages 359–374, 2007.
3. S. Chiasson, A. Forget, R. Biddle, and P. C. Van Oorschot. Influencing users towards better passwords: Persuasive cued click-points. *British Computer Society Conference on Human-Computer Interaction*, 1:121–130, 2008.

4. S-B. Cho. Neural-network classifiers for recognizing totally unconstrained handwritten numerals. *IEEE Trans. on Neural Networks*, 8:43–53, 1997.
5. D. Davis, F. Monrose, and M. K. Reiter. On user choice in graphical password schemes. *Proc. of the 13th USENIX Security Symposium*, pages 151–164, 2004.
6. A. De Angeli, L. Coventry, G. Johnson, and K. Renaud. Is a picture really worth a thousand words? exploring the feasibility of graphical authentication systems. *Int'l Journal of Human Computer Studies*, 63(1–2):128–152, 2005.
7. R. Dhamija and A. Perrig. Déjà vu: A user study using images for authentication. *Proc. of the 9th USENIX Security Symposium*, pages 45–58, 2000.
8. P. Dunphy and J. Yan. Do background images improve "draw a secret" graphical passwords? *Proc. of the 14th ACM Conf. on Computer and Communications Security*, pages 36–47, 2007.
9. M. Faundez-Zanuy. Signature Recognition State-of-the-art. *IEEE Aerospace and Electronic Systems Magazine*, pages 28–32, July 2005.
10. M. Fuandez-Zanuy. Biometric Security Technology. *IEEE Aerospace and Electronic Systems Magazine*, 21(6):15–26, June 2006.
11. Y. Gao and M. K. H. Leung. Face recognition using line edge map. *IEEE Transactions on Pattern Analysis and Machine Intelligence*, 24:764–779, 2002.
12. H. Gao, X. Guo, X. Chen, L. Wang, and X. Liu. Yet another graphical password strategy. *Proc. of the Annual Computer Security Applications Conference*, pages 121–129, 2008.
13. C. Geng and X. Jiang. Face recognition using sift features. *16th IEEE Int'l Conf. on Image Processing*, pages 3313–3316, 2009.
14. J. Goldberg and J. Hagman. Doodling our way to better authentication. *Proc. of the ACM Conference on Human Factors in Computing Systems*, pages 868–869, 2002.
15. D. S. Guru and H. N. Prakash. Online Signature Verification and Recognition: An Approach Based on Symbolic Representation. *IEEE Transactions on Pattern Analysis and Machine Intelligence*, 31(6):1059–1073, June 2009.
16. M. Hamdani, A.E.-D. Mousa, and H. Ney. Open vocabulary arabic handwriting recognition using morphologycal decomposition. *Int'l Conf. on Document Analysis and Recogntion*, pages 280–284, 2013.
17. N. M. Herbst and C. N. Liu. Signature verification method and apparatus utilizing both acceleration and pressure characteristics. *U.S. Patent 4 128 829*, 1978.
18. G. F. Houle, D. B. Aragon, R. W. Smith, M. Shridhar, and D. Kimura. A multi-layered corroboration based check reader. In J. J. Hull and S. L. Taylor, editors, *Document Analysis System II*, pages 137–174. World Scientific, 1998.
19. A. Jain, L. Hong, and Y. Kulkarni. A multimodal biometric system using fingerprint, face, and speech. *2nd Int'l Conf. on AVBPA*, pages 182–187, 1999.
20. A. K. Jain, F. D. Griess, and S. D. Connell. On-line signature verification. *Pattern Recognition*, 35:2963–2972, 2002.
21. A. K. Jain, A. Ross, and S. Prabhakar. An introduction to biometric recognition. *IEEE Trans. on Circuits and Systems for Video Technology*, 14(1):4–20, Jan. 2004.
22. I. Jermyn, A. Mayer, F. Monrose, M. Reiter, and A. Rubin. The design and analysis of graphical passwords. *Proc. of the 8th USENIX Security Symposium*, pages 1–14, 1999.
23. R. S. Kashi, Jianying Hu, and W. L. Nelson. On-line handwritten signature verification using hidden markov model features. *Proc. of the 4th Int'l. Conf. on Document Analysis and Recognition*, 1:253–257, 1997.
24. C. Kaufman, R. Perlman, and M. Speciner. *Network security: private communication in a public world*. Prentice Hall, 2nd edition, 2002.
25. A. Kholmatov and B. Yanikoglu. Identity authentication using improved online signature verification method. *Pattern Recognition Letters*, 26:2400–2408, 2005.
26. A. Kosmala, J. Rottland, and G. Rigoll. An investigation of the use of trigraphs for large vocabulary cursive handwriting recognition. *IEEE Int'l Conf. on Acoustics, Speech, and Signal Processing*, pages 3373–3376, 1997.
27. C. Liu, F. Yin, Q. Wang, and D. Wang. Icdar 2011 chinese handwriting recognition competition. *Int'l Conf. on Document Analysis and Recognition*, pages 1464–1469, 2011.

28. D. Maltoni, D. Maio, A. K. Jain, and S. Prabhakar. *Handbook of fingerprint recognition.* Springer, Berlin, 2003.
29. M. M. Mehdi. Optimized word segmentation for the word based cursive handwriting recognition. *2013 European Modelling Symposium*, pages 299–304, 2013.
30. A. Nagar, K. Nandakumar, and A. K. Jain. Multibiometric cryptosystem based on feature level fusion. *IEEE Trans. on Information Forensics and Security*, 7(1):255–268, 2012.
31. PASSFACES CORPORATION. The science behind passfaces. http://www.passfaces.com/published/The%20Science%20Behind%20Passfaces.pdf, 2009.
32. H. Pesch, J. Hamdani, M. Forster, and H. Ney. Analysis of preprocessing techniques for latin handwriting recognition. *Int'l Conf. on Frontiers in Handwriting Recognition*, pages 280–284, 2012.
33. R. Plamondon and G. Lorette. Automatic Signature Verification and Write Identification—The State of the Art. *Pattern Recognition*, 22(2):107–131, 1989.
34. N. K. Rantha, S. Chikkerur, J. H. Connell, and R. M. Bolle. Generating cancelable fingerprint templates. *IEEE Trans. on Pattern Analysis and Machine Intelligence*, 29(4), April 2007.
35. K. V. Renaud. Guidelines for designing graphical authentication mechanism interfaces. *Int'l Journal of Information and Computer Security*, 3(1):60–85, 2009.
36. K. V. Renaud. On user involvement in production of images used in visual authentication. *Journal of Visual Languages & Computing*, 20(1):1–15, 2009.
37. A. Ross and A. K. Jain. Multimodal biometrics: an overview. *Proc. of 12th EUSIPCO*, pages 1221–1224, 2004.
38. A. Ross, K. Nandakumar, and A. K. Jain. *Handbook of multi biometrics.* Spinger-Verlag, New York, 2006.
39. M. Savvides, B. V. K. Vijaya Kumar, and P. K. Khosla. Cancelable biometric filters for face recognition. *Procs of the 17Th. Int'l Conf. on Pattern Recognition*, pages 922–925, August 2004.
40. Y. Taigman, M. Yang, M. Ranzato, and L. Wolf. Deepface: closing the gap to human-level performance in face verification. *IEEE Conf. on Computer Vision and Pattern Recognition*, pages 1701–1708, 2014.
41. H. Tao and C. Adams. Pass-go: A proposal to improve the usability of graphical passwords. *Int'l Journal of Network Security*, 7(2):273–292, 2008.
42. C. Varenhorst. Passdoodles: A lightweight authentication method. *MIT Research Science Institute*, July 2004.
43. S. Weidenbeck, J. Waters, J. Birget, A. Brodskiy, and N. Memon. Authentication using graphical passwords: Basic results. *Proc. of the 11th Int'l Conf. on Human-Computer Interaction*, 2005.
44. S. Weidenbeck, J. Waters, J. Birget, A. Brodskiy, and N. Memon. Authentication using graphical passwords: Effects of tolerance and image choice. *Proc. of the 1st Symposium on Usable Privacy and Security*, pages 1–12, 2005.
45. S. Weidenbeck, J. Waters, J. Birget, A. Brodskiy, and N. Memon. Passpoints: Design and longitudinal evaluation of a graphical password system. *Int'l Journal of Human Computer Studies*, 63(1–2):102–127, 2005.
46. F. Yin, Q. Wang, and X. Zhang. Icdar 2013 chinese handwriting recognition competition. *Int'l Conf. on Document Analysis and Recognition*, pages 1464–1470, 2013.
47. H. Zhou, A. Mian, L. Wei, and D. Creighton. Recent advances on single modal and multimodal face recognition: a survey. *IEEE Transactions on Human-Machine Systems*, PP(99):1–16, 2014.

Chapter 3
Sketch-Based Authentication

Abstract This chapter considers two different recognition/matching algorithms, namely dynamic time warping (DTW) and Simple K-Space (SKS). Both algorithms utilize classical pattern recognition techniques to the novel application of sketch-based password. While more sophisticated techniques are possible, DTW and SKS are chosen because the inherent nature of the underlying problem is easily perceived using the approaches. Plus, the fundamental concepts discussed in the chapter generalize beyond the specific algorithmic implementation. The overall sketch-based authentication framework is outlined in this chapter using DTW and SKS. The respective implementation details are rigorously discussed, from which the philosophies are compared and contrasted. In particular, these methods have a similar objective, but different parameterizations, operating spaces, and computational complexities.

Keywords DTW · SKS · Correspondence · Density estimation · Sketch · Authentication

In this chapter, two contrasting models, namely dynamic time warping (DTW) and Simple K-Space (SKS) for recognizing sketch-based passwords are discussed. DTW was originally used for optimal alignment of phonemes in voice recognition applications, and later extended to signature recognition (see [3]). SKS was originally applied to shape recognition [11], and later extended to image registration [8].

The two approaches have a similar objective, which is to determine the minimum (maximum) dissimilarity (similarity) between two parameterized curves (e.g. voice signal, signature, or even a sketch). However, the major differences between DTW and SKS include: (1) parameterization, (2) operating space, and (3) search-time complexity. Each method is discussed in detail, specifically in regard to the application of sketch-based passwords.

3.1 Dynamic Time Warping

Consider two continuous sketch-based passwords, $\alpha^* : I \rightarrow \mathbb{R}^d$ and $\beta^* : I \rightarrow \mathbb{R}^d$, defined by $\alpha^*(t) = (\alpha^{(1)}, , \alpha^{(2)}, \ldots, \alpha^{(d)})$ and $\beta^*(t) = (\beta^{(1)}, , \beta^{(2)}, \ldots, \beta^{(d)})$ for all $t \in I$, where I is the interval $(0, 1)$ *without loss of generality.* and d is the dimensionality (i.e. $d = 2$ for planar sketches or $d = 3$ for sketches or gestures in 3D).

© The Author(s) 2014
B. S. Riggan et al., *Fundamentals of Sketch-Based Passwords,*
SpringerBriefs in Computer Science, DOI 10.1007/978-3-319-13629-5_3

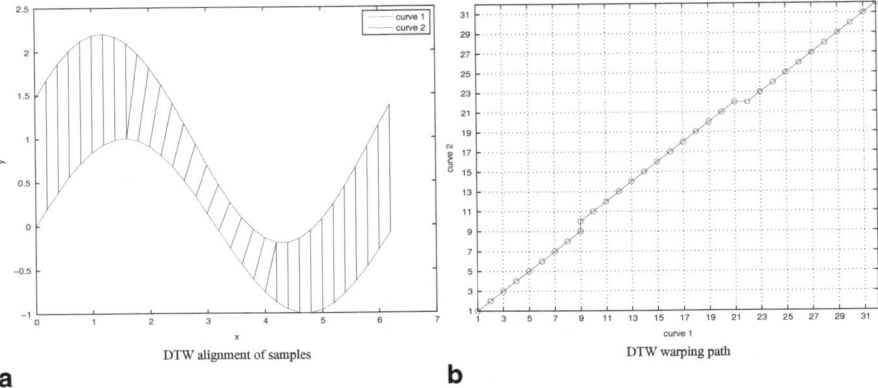

Fig. 3.1 Example DTW alignment and correspondence path. (Refer to the online version for color plots)

Practically, most methods do not explicitly operate on the continuous sketches; discrete approximations are usually used. Therefore, the sketches, α^* and β^*, may be represented as $\mathbf{X} = [\mathbf{x}_1 \, \mathbf{x}_2 \, \cdots \, \mathbf{x}_n] \in \mathbb{R}^{d \times n}$ and $\mathbf{Y} = [\mathbf{y}_1 \, \mathbf{y}_2 \, \cdots \, \mathbf{y}_m] \in \mathbb{R}^{d \times m}$ respectively, where $\mathbf{x}_i = i \Delta t_x$ and $\mathbf{y}_j = j \Delta t_y$, assuming (fixed or variable) sampling intervals, Δt_x and Δt_y.

The objective of DTW is to optimally align the samples of $\mathbf{X}$ and $\mathbf{Y}$ (see example sample alignment in Fig. 3.1a) Intuitively, this means finding the warping path or correspondence path (Fig. 3.1b), $\Omega = [\omega_x^* \, \omega_y^*]^T \in \mathbb{R}^{2 \times k}$, that minimizes the following objective function[1]

$$J(\Omega) = \sum_{i=1}^{k} \left\| \mathbf{x}_{\omega xi} - \mathbf{y}_{\omega yi} \right\|^2 \qquad (3.1)$$

such that the warping path adheres to the following constraints:

1. **boundary**—$[\omega_{x1} \, \omega_{y1}]^T = [1 \ 1]^T$ and $[\omega_{xk} \, \omega_{yk}]^T = [n \ m]^T$
2. **monotonic**—$\|[\omega_{xj} \, \omega_{yj}]^T\| \geq \|[\omega_{xi} \, \omega_{yi}]^T\|$ for all $j \geq i$
3. **continous** (i.e. connected)—$0 \leq \|[\omega_{xi} \, \omega_{yi}]^T - [\omega_{x(i-1)} \, \omega_{y(i-1)}]^T\|_1 \leq 2$

Zhou and De la Torre [12] showed that Eq. 3.1 is equivalent to Eq. 3.2 below.

$$J(\mathbf{W}_x, \mathbf{W}_y) = \left\| \mathbf{X}\mathbf{W}_x^T - \mathbf{Y}\mathbf{W}_y^T \right\|_F^2 \qquad (3.2)$$

$\mathbf{W}_x$ and $\mathbf{W}_y$, which are used to encode the warping path Ω, represent matrices of sizes $k \times n$ and $k \times m$ respectively. This optimization problem is typically solved using dynamic programming [2] in $O(nm)$ time. In some cases, this computational

---

[1] $k = min\{n, m\}$ is the number points necessary to align the sketches.

complexity may be reduced by imposing additional constraints, e.g. slope constraints, global path constraints, and slope weighting. However, these additional constraints may lead to sub-optimal results.

Alternatively, [13] proposed a generalized time warping (GTW) method that can solve the DTW optimization problem in $O(dke + e^3)$ (where e denotes the number of basis functions for approximating the warping path), which is generally more efficient than the dynamic programming approach. Assuming $d \ll n, m$ and a "small" number of basis functions, then the complexity of the GTW is more efficient than the traditional dynamic programming approach.

The primary assumption enabling a reduction in computational complexity is representing the warping path as a linear combination of monotonic basis functions.

While solving the aforementioned optimization problem is useful for DTW, it is not the only objective. The overall objective of DTW is to determine the minimum dissimilarity between two given sketches, which are parameterized by time. Finding the optimal warping path is a critical component of this process because, after optimization, Ω aligns the samples of $\mathbf{X}$ and $\mathbf{Y}$ such that minimum dissimilarity, $J(\cdot)$, between the two is achieved.

Until now, in this chapter, DTW has only considered the alignment between two individual sketches. In the context of sketch-based authentication, both enrollment and login cases must be considered when implementing a DTW-based approach.

During enrollment, a user is expected to provide multiple instances of a sketch-based password; preferably a distinct and memorable one. Multiple sketches are required to capture some of the variations in the "password." This is, in fact, similar to text-based passwords, where a user is expected to enter his/her password at least twice. Therefore, it is not unreasonable to demand multiple sketch-based passwords during enrollment.

There are at least two ways to enroll a sketch-based password: (1) construct a representative sketch by aligning every exemplar or (2) retain all the sketches (or a subset of them) provided during enrollment and align any login sketch with every enrolled sketch. This first case requires a lot of computation up front, and the second postpones the computation until login time. Overall, the latter is more computationally efficient. For example, assuming c exemplars, the computational complexities of the respective methods are $O(c^2nm)$ and $O(cnm)$. Therefore, the login phase is discussed assuming the latter enrollment approach.

During login, a sketch is compared with c exemplar sketch-based passwords of the specified user[2]. In other words, the login sketch is optimally aligned with each of the c exemplars using DTW. This process yield c different dissimilarity values (or distances) $\{d_i\}_{i=1}^c$. The sketch-based password is considered to be of the same type if the average distance is sufficiently "small", i.e. $\frac{1}{c} \sum_{i=1}^c d_i < \varepsilon$.

---

[2] Here, the verification problem is assumed in application to authentication systems.

3.2 Simple K-Space

Simple K-Space (SKS), instead, attempts to determine the maximum similarity between two sketches using a probabilistic framework. Some notable differences between SKS and DTW include the parameterization, operating space, and computational complexity. Before discussing SKS in detail, a brief review of kernel density estimation is required.

3.2.1 Kernel Density Estimation

Given a set of samples, $\{\mathbf{v}_i\}_{i=1}^n$ where $\mathbf{v}_i \in \mathbb{R}^d$, from an unknown multivariate probability distribution $p(\mathbf{v})$, the goal of kernel density estimation is to approximate the unknown distribution. The estimation of the underlying distribution is:

$$\hat{p}(\mathbf{v}) = \frac{1}{n} \sum_{i=1}^n \frac{1}{|\mathbf{H}|} \phi \left(\mathbf{H}^{-1}(\mathbf{v} - \mathbf{v}_i) \right) \tag{3.3}$$

where the kernel function $\phi(\cdot)$, with bandwidth parameter $\mathbf{H}$, is a non-negative, real valued function that satisfies the following:

$$\int_{\mathbb{R}^d} \phi(\mathbf{u}) \, d\mathbf{u} = 1$$

and

$$\phi(-\mathbf{u}) = \phi(\mathbf{u}).$$

A 1D example of kernel density estimation is shown in Fig. 3.2. In the subsequent sections, the relationship between multivariate density estimation and the SKS model is demonstrated. Therefore, keep this simple example when mind when attempting to comprehend the concept of the SKS model.

3.2.2 Model

Now, the SKS model representation, which exhibits similarities to kernel density estimation (Sect. 3.2.1) and Kendall's [7] shape space, may be discussed in detail. The biggest difference between SKS and Kendall's [6, 7] representation of shape is SKS constructs a translation and rotation invariant descriptor (after accounting for scale variations), whereas Kendall constructs a translation and scale invariant "pre-shape" and accounts for any rotation. First, the 2D model representation, originally applied in shape recognition applications, is presented. Then, the SKS model is generalized to a model with an arbitrary number of dimensions.

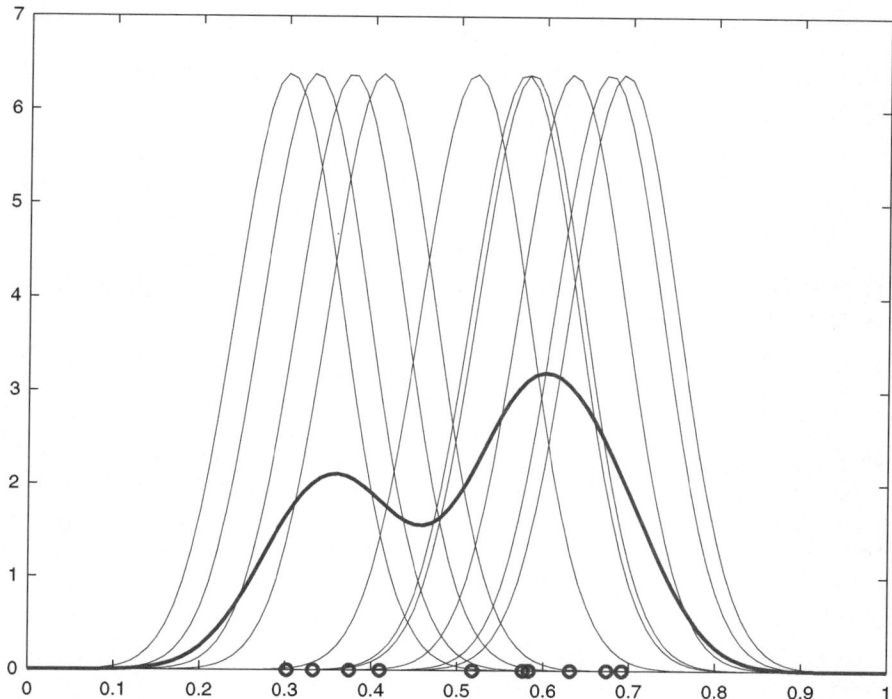

Fig. 3.2 The "circles" on the horizontal axis mark the sample points from the underlying distribution. The *thin curves* (in *blue*) represent the individual kernels, i.e. Gaussians, corresponding to each sample point. The *thick curve* (in *red*) represents the estimated probability density function. (Refer to the online version for color plots)

3.2.2.1 2D Model

From now on, assume than any sketch (continuous or discrete) is assumed to be planar (i.e. d = 2). For notation purposes, this implies that $\alpha^*(t) = (\alpha^{(1)}(t), \alpha^{(2)}(t)) = (x(t), y(t))$ for the continuous case, and $\mathbf{x}_i = (x_i, y_i)$ for the discrete.

Let a discrete sketch, $\mathbf{X} = [\mathbf{x}_1 \, \mathbf{x}_2 \, \cdots \, \mathbf{x}_n]$, be sampled with respect to time, as in Sect. 3.1. In order to construct a time invariant representation, $\mathbf{X}$ is first resampled with respect to arc length. Arc length reparameterization in the continuous domain provides a sketch (or curve) that is unit speed, i.e. $\left\| \frac{d\alpha^*}{dt}(t) \right\| = 1 \quad \forall t$. In the discrete domain, resampling with respect to arc length provides a sketch with (approximately) equidistant samples. The discrete resampling procedure requires an interpolation of the sketch. For a review on interpolation and resampling, refer to Appendix 1.

Given a discrete sketch, $\hat{\mathbf{X}}$, assumed to be resampled with respect to arc length, a translation and rotation invariant representation can be constructed by computing a distance-curvature pair, (ρ_i, κ_i) for every $\hat{\mathbf{x}}_i$. $\rho_i = \|\hat{\mathbf{x}}_i - \hat{\mathbf{x}}_0\|$ represents the distance between the ith sample point and an arbitrary, but constant, reference point[3] $\hat{\mathbf{x}}_0$, and κ_i represents the local curvature at the ith sample point.

Curvature, in the continuous domain, for a sketch, $\alpha^*(t)$ parameterized by time is defined as

$$\kappa(t) = \frac{\frac{\partial \alpha^*}{\partial x}(t)\frac{\partial^2 \alpha^*}{\partial y^2}(t) - \frac{\partial^2 \alpha^*}{\partial x^2}(t)\frac{\partial \alpha^*}{\partial y}(t)}{\left(\left(\frac{\partial \alpha^*}{\partial x}(t)\right) + \left(\frac{\partial \alpha^*}{\partial y}(t)\right)\right)^{\frac{3}{2}}} \tag{3.4}$$

If a continuous curve is unit speed, then an alternative definition is the magnitude of the derivative of the unit tangent vector, or

$$\kappa(s) = \left\|\frac{\partial^2 \alpha^*}{\partial s^2}\right\| \tag{3.5}$$

where s denotes arc length. However, in the case of discrete sketches (sampled with respect to either time or arc length), curvature must be approximated. There are many approaches to estimating curvature. For a specific implementation details, see Appendix 2.

Now,

$$\mathbf{V} = \begin{bmatrix} \rho_1 & \rho_2 & \cdots & \rho_n \\ \kappa_1 & \kappa_2 & \cdots & \kappa_n \end{bmatrix}$$

provides a representation that is invariant to translations and rotations. In order to achieve invariance to scale, the sketch must be normalized to unity scale prior to mapping from the input space to the feature space. After centering the points, a sketch is normalized to unity scale by dividing each point the scale factor, defined by

$$\gamma = \frac{1}{n}\sum_{i=1}^{n}\mathbf{x}_i - \mathbf{x}_0 \tag{3.6}$$

which is similar to kendall's definition of scale (c.f. [7]).

Given the invariant representation $\mathbf{V}$, assumed to be normalized to unity scale, the 2D SKS model is defined as

$$m(\rho,\kappa) = \sum_{i=1}^{n}\exp\left(-\frac{1}{2}\left(\frac{(\rho-\rho_i)^2}{\sigma_1^2} + \frac{(\kappa-\kappa_i)^2}{\sigma_2^2}\right)\right) \tag{3.7}$$

where σ_1 and σ_2 are the bandwidth parameters, which are used for smoothing the model, for ρ and κ respectively.

---

[3] Usually $\hat{\mathbf{x}}_0$ is the center of gravity, but this is not a requirement. However, it does reduce the computational complexity later.

Note the similarity between the model (Eq. 3.7) and the kernel density estimator in Eq. 3.3. The relationship between the probability, $\hat{p}(\rho, \kappa)$, and the model, $m(\rho, \kappa)$, is

$$\hat{p}(\rho, \kappa) = \frac{1}{2\pi n \sigma_1 \sigma_2} m(\rho, \kappa),$$

assuming the bandwidth parameter

$$\mathbf{H} = \begin{bmatrix} \sigma_1 & 0 \\ 0 & \sigma_2 \end{bmatrix}.$$

Therefore, the SKS model is similar to a density estimation over the feature space of the sketch.

It is important to recognize the function $m : \mathbb{R}^2 \rightarrow \mathbb{R}$ describes a surface over a 2D feature space representing the distribution of features. The scalar value, $m(\rho, \kappa)$, is considered a likelihood measure that there exists a point along the sketch that lies a distance ρ from the reference and has a local curvature of κ.

> **Remark 3.1** Although the sketch samples are explicitly ordered, the SKS model does not preserve this ordering of the samples. Therefore, the 2D SKS model is ideal for representing the shape of a set of points since a change in sample order does not affect the shape of collection of points.

3.2.2.2 Generalized Model

The SKS framework may be generalized to an arbitrary number of dimensions in the features space. Now, consider the invariant representation of $\mathbf{X}$ to be composed of a distance and a $\ell - 1$ dimensional feature vector. That is,

$$\mathbf{V} = \begin{bmatrix} \mathbf{v}_1 & \mathbf{v}_2 & \cdots & \mathbf{v}_n \end{bmatrix} = \begin{bmatrix} \rho_1 & \rho_2 & \cdots & \rho_n \\ \kappa_1^* & \kappa_2^* & \cdots & \kappa_n^* \end{bmatrix} \in \mathbb{R}^{\ell \times n} \qquad (3.8)$$

In general, for invariance to be achieved all features must move (i.e. translate, rotate, and scale) with the sketch. Similar to Eq. 3.7, the generalized SKS model $m : \mathbb{R}^\ell \rightarrow \mathbb{R}$ is defined as

$$m(\mathbf{v}) = \sum_{i=1}^{n} \exp\left(-\frac{1}{2}(\mathbf{v} - \mathbf{v}_i)^T \Sigma^{-1} (\mathbf{v} - \mathbf{v}_i)\right), \qquad (3.9)$$

where Σ is a symmetric, positive-definite matrix which is used to smooth the SKS model. Typically, Σ is assumed to be a diagonal matrix, implying that the model is smoothed independently in each feature direction. However, in general, this feature dependency must be considered for a more accurate estimation/representation.

Clearly, by letting $\mathbf{v} = (\rho, \kappa)$, $\mathbf{v}_i = (\rho_i, \kappa_i)$, and $\Sigma = \mathrm{diag}(\sigma_1, \sigma_2)$, the original SKS model (Eq. 3.7) is a special case of the generalized SKS model (Eq. 3.9).

As with the 2D model, the generalized model describes a hyper-surface over a ℓD feature space representing the distribution of the feature vectors over the sketch. Likewise, the scalar value, $m(\mathbf{v})$ in Eq. 3.9, represents the likelihood that there exists a point over the sketch with the properties defined by $\mathbf{v}$.

In regards to order, the sample order, in general, may either be preserved or ignored, depending on the application. This point is discussed further in Chapter 5.

3.2.3 Accumulator

The overall objective is to determine whether or not two sketch-based passwords are similar enough to be considered the "same." As mentioned previously, SKS determines the maximum similarity between two sketches in order to make such a determination.

The concept of similarity in the SKS framework is posed as the summation of similarity evidence, which may be captured by an accumulator (c.f. [1]). Given the generalized SKS model, $m(\mathbf{v})$, of an exemplar sketch $\mathbf{X}$ and a test sketch $\mathbf{Y} = [\mathbf{y}_1 \, \mathbf{y}_2 \, \cdots \, \mathbf{y}_n]$ (with corresponding features $\kappa_1^*, \ldots, \kappa_n^*$), the accumulator is defined as

$$A(\hat{\mathbf{y}}) = \sum_{i=1}^{n} m(\hat{\mathbf{y}} - \mathbf{y}_i, \kappa^*). \qquad (3.10)$$

Example accumulators (one that indicates a matching sketch, and one that indicates a non-matching sketch) are shown in Fig. 3.3.

For a given estimated reference point of $\mathbf{Y}$, denoted as $\hat{\mathbf{y}}$, the accumulator value represents the similarity between the features of $\mathbf{X}$ and the features of $\mathbf{Y}$ (conditioned on $\hat{\mathbf{y}}$). In other words, the accumulator simultaneously determines how consistent a sketch $\mathbf{Y}$ (with reference $\hat{\mathbf{y}}$) is with the model of $\mathbf{X}$ and whether $\hat{\mathbf{y}}$ is a sufficiently "good" reference for the sketch. Therefore, the goal of SKS is to determine

$$A_{max} = \max_{\hat{\mathbf{y}}} A(\hat{\mathbf{y}}), \qquad (3.11)$$

which directly aligns with the previously stated objective: *finding the maximum similarity between two sketches.*

3.2.4 Decision Thresholding

The last step in order to determine if a sketch is sufficiently consistent with model of another sketch, implying similarity between the sketches, is thresholding. If

Fig. 3.3 Examples accumulators which indicate sketches (**a**) a matching sketch and (**b**) non-matching sketch respectively. (Note the test sketches are overlaid on top of the respective accumulators. Images are best viewed in color (see online version))

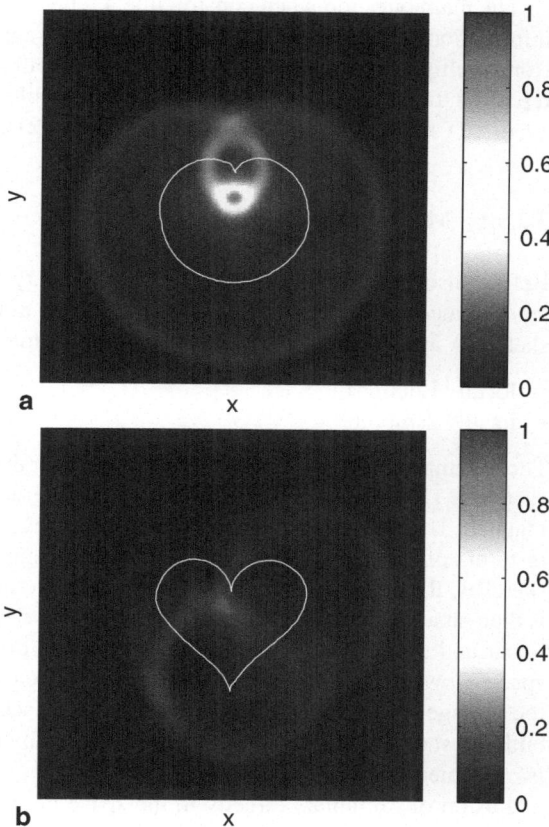

$A_{max} > \epsilon$, then the sketch is considered to match the exemplar sketch, indicating access is *granted*; otherwise, the sketch is considered to be different, meaning access is *denied*. This type of decision thresholding is similar to that for DTW, except the direction of the of inequality.

3.2.5   Representative Model

Similar to DTW, SKS is only defined as a comparison mechanism for two sketches. As with DTW, there are two approaches for enrollment: (1) construct a model that is representative of the exemplars provided, or (2) construct a model for each of the example sketches provided during enrollment (and compare a login sketch with every model). Since the latter approach was discussed using DTW, the former is discussed here.

The main question when constructing a representative model is: how to combine information from each sketch? There are many approaches for fusing information from multiple exemplars, e.g. optimization methods, dictionary learning, sparse representations, etc., but there are only two possible spaces in which this fusion may occur: (1) space of sketches, or (2) space of models.

3.2.5.1 Manifold Assumption

Before discussing fusion methods, it is necessary that in most cases the sketches are assumed to lie on some manifold in a high dimensional space. The "space of sketches" are assumed to have the properties of manifold:

- locally Euclidean
- locally "smooth"

The assumption is that sketches input by the user during enrollment must be similar sketches. This means the sketches must be of the same shape and drawn in a similar manner. Therefore, on the manifold of sketches, they are considered to be close in terms of their geodesic distance. Since the models are constructed from these sketches, they too lie in "close" proximity on the manifold of models. The average is then an adequate representative model for the class because manifolds are locally linear and the average optimally minimizes the distance from each point in linear space. However, if a user enters extremely different sketches during enrollment then the average model is a poor representative of the set of sketches. Therefore, a simple outlier test to determine if the sketches provided by the user are sufficiently different is implemented.

Fusion of exemplars directly in the space of sketches appears to be simple and intuitive. However, we can show that this approach is actually constructing a representation, which is not desired. Consider the collection of exemplars sketches, $\{^i\mathbf{X}\}_{i=1}^c$. Fusion in this manner may be mathematically described as

$$\bar{\mathbf{V}} = [\bar{\mathbf{v}}_1 \ \bar{\mathbf{v}}_2 \ \cdots \ \bar{\mathbf{v}}_n]$$

$$= \sum_{i=1}^c {}^i\mathbf{V}$$

$$= \sum_{i=1}^c \left[{}^i\mathbf{v}_1 \ {}^i\mathbf{v}_2 \ \cdots {}^i\mathbf{v}_n \right],$$

where $^i\mathbf{V}$ is the corresponding invariant representation of $^i\mathbf{X}$. From $\bar{\mathbf{V}}$, a representative model could be computed as

$$m(\bar{\mathbf{v}}) = \sum_{i=1}^n \exp\left(-\frac{1}{2}(\bar{\mathbf{v}} - \bar{\mathbf{v}}_i)^T \Sigma^{-1} (\bar{\mathbf{v}} - \bar{\mathbf{v}}_i) \right) \tag{3.12}$$

Fig. 3.4 Computing the representative model for a set of input sketches. The nodes on the *left* represent the individual models constructed from the input sketches and the output node symbolizes the representative model

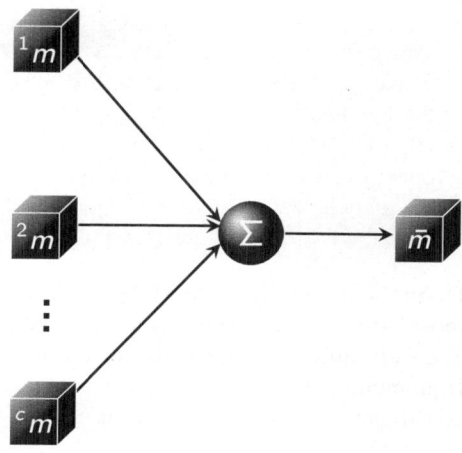

Note that this distribution differs from that in Eq. 3.9 because the value $m(\bar{\mathbf{v}})$ represents a likelihood measurement that the feature vector sum, $\bar{\mathbf{v}}$, occurs over the collection of sketches. This representation is a distribution of element-wise sums of features, which is not exactly what we wish to model because the sketch alignment may be significantly different (even when reparameterized with arc length). Therefore, the feature sums may not necessarily be representative for the typical sketch.

Alternatively, consider the collection of individual models, $\left\{{}^{i}m(\mathbf{v})\right\}_{i=1}^{c}$, where

$$ {}^{i}m(\mathbf{v}) = \sum_{j=1}^{n} \exp\left(-\frac{1}{2}(\mathbf{v} - {}^{i}\mathbf{v}_j)^T \Sigma^{-1}(\mathbf{v} - {}^{i}\mathbf{v}_j)\right) \tag{3.13} $$

A representative model can be constructed by summing the models directly (Fig. 3.4), i.e. $\bar{m}(\mathbf{v}) = \sum_{i=1}^{c} {}^{i}m(\mathbf{v})$. This model representation constructs a distribution from the individual features (opposed to feature sums) from the collection of sketches. Equivalently, let the features from the collection of sketches be denoted as $\{\mathbf{v}_\tau\}_{\tau=1}^{c}$, and then the representative model may be defined as:

$$ \bar{m}(\mathbf{v}) = \sum_{\tau=1}^{nc} \exp\left((\mathbf{v} - \mathbf{v}_\tau)^T \Sigma^{-1}(\mathbf{v} - \mathbf{v}_\tau)\right) $$

which is very similar to Eq. 3.9, except for the number of elements being summed.

Remark 3.2 If $\{\mathbf{v}_\tau\}_{\tau=1}^{nc}$ is considered to be a larger collection of features for the same class (i.e. a sketch-based password for particular user), then the model estimate, $\bar{m}(\mathbf{v})$, is improved from the estimate obtain using a single sketch (with n sample points). Knowing that a kernel density estimation, $\hat{p}(\mathbf{v})$ converges to the "true" probability density $p(\mathbf{v})$ as the $n \rightarrow \infty$ (provided that the bandwidth inversely scales with n), a similar argument can be made in regard to $\bar{m}(\mathbf{v})$ because of the relationship between the SKS model and kernel density estimation. Essentially, more information provides a better estimate of the model.

During login, the consistency between a given login sketch and the representative model is computed using the same accumulative technique discuss in Sect. 3.2.3. The only difference is the use of the representative model, which is constructed from multiple instances of a sketch-based password, rather than a particular model, constructed from a single instance.

3.2.6 Compare and Contrast

While DTW and SKS have similar objectives related to determining the dissimilarity/similarity between sketch-based passwords, they have contrasting perspectives and implementations. These differences include varying parameterizations, operating spaces, and computational complexities.

First, both methods ultimately seek a time-invariant representation. DTW achieves time invariance by finding the optimal set of correspondences in order to make the best possible comparison between two sketches. Whereas, SKS reparameterizes each sketch by arc length in order to produce a time invariant representation. The trade-off is finding correspondence requires more computation up front, but may find an optimal alignment. However, reparameterization requires an efficient resampling procedure, but the ith sample of reparameterized sketch may not accurately correspond in terms of feature similarity (as with DTW).

Second, DTW operates directly on the sketches, and SKS maps the sketches to an invariant representation. The difference is that DTW directly attempts to minimized the "error," and SKS attempts to reduces the search space by removing trivial transformations (e.g. translations, rotation, and scale). Additionally, SKS attempts to construct a density-like model where a probabilistic type of analysis may be used.

Finally, the computational complexities for comparing a testing sketch with a set of c exemplars using DTW and SKS are approximately $O(cn^2)$ and $O((c+size(A))n)$ respectively. Note, the assumption here is that all exemplars and test sketches have n samples. Also, $size(A)$ denotes the number of points computed in the accumulator, which typically a small number of points within a "small" neighborhood around the center of gravity (i.e. the expect reference) of the test sketch.

3.3   Key Points

The primary observations from this chapter include:

1. DTW attempts to optimally align sketch samples based on feature dissimilarity.
2. DTW uses dynamic programming to find the minimum dissimilarity between sketches.
3. SKS attempts to determine the maximum similarity between sketches.
4. SKS is similar a multivariate kernel density estimator, except that the SKS model does not integrate to unity.
5. The SKS framework extended to an arbitrary number of sketch properties, including biometrics.
6. There are two ways to compare a test sketch with multiple sketches: (1) determine similarity of a test sketch with all representatives, or constructed an "average" representation from exemplars (and make only one comparison).
7. DTW achieves time invariance by find corresponding samples; SKS reparameterizes with respect to arc length.
8. DTW operates directly on the sketches; SKS constructs an invariant representation.
9. DTW computational complexity is $O(n^2)$ for a single comparison; SKS is $O((size(A) + 1)n)$.

Appendix 1

Resampling the sketches is a critical implementation detail that is sometime overlooked in sketch-based authentication. In this appendix, both linear and cubic interpolation methods are discussed for resampling. While there are many other methods of interpolation, these are simple, efficient, and sufficiently accurate for the purposes of this brief.

Linear Interpolation

A trivial solution is to use a linear interpolant to determine the unknown points around the sketch. Linear interpolation uses a two point neighborhood since two points are necessary for determining the equation of a line. Given that $t \in [t_i, t_{i+1}]$, then the interpolation is computed using

$$f(t) = a_1 \left(\frac{t - t_i}{t_{i+1} - t_i} \right) + a_0$$

where

$$a_1 = -\frac{1}{2} f(t_i) + \frac{1}{2} f(t_{i+1})$$

$$a_0 = f(t_i)$$

Table 3.1 A comparison of different ordered interpolations

Interpolant	First derivative	Second derivative	Curvature
L	Constant	–	–
Quadratic	1st order	Constant	Piecewise constant
Cubic	2nd order	1st	Piecewise linear
n^{th} order	$n-1$ order	$n-2$ order	Piecewise $n-2$ order

Fig. 3.5 Cubic interpolation
of a one parameter function

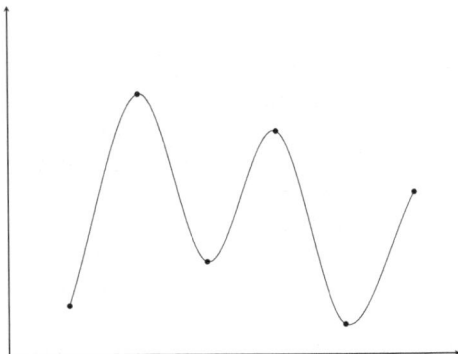

and $\{(f(t_i), t_i), (f(t_{i+1}), t_{i+1})\}$ is the two point neighborhood of ith discrete sample point on the sketch.

Linear interpolation is a quick and easy solution, but it is not very accurate when considering the nonlinearity of many sketches. More importantly, since curvature (i.e. a second derivative) is used in the recognition algorithm, this implies that linear interpolation only yields curvature information at points between two different interpolants. Therefore, a higher order interpolation is necessary. Table 3.1 provides information about various higher order interpolants for purposes of comparison (Fig. 3.5).

Cubic Interpolation

Cubic interpolation usually provides a better representation of the continuous sketch than linear interpolation, but one danger is possible overfitting. Also, curvature information exists at all interpolated points due to the use of a third order interpolant (twice differentiable). Cubic interpolation uses a 4 point local neighborhood (opposed to a 2 point neighborhood for linear interpolation) to determine the interpolant between the two center points in the neighborhood. The interpolant formula for $t \in [t_i, t_{i+1}]$ is

$$f(t) = a_3 \left(\frac{t - t_i}{t_{i+1} - t_i} \right)^3 + a_2 \left(\frac{t - t_i}{t_{i+1} - t_i} \right)^2 + a_1 \left(\frac{t - t_i}{t_{i+1} - t_i} \right) + a_0$$

where

$$a_3 = -\frac{1}{2}f(t_{i-1}) + \frac{3}{2}f(t_i) - \frac{3}{2}f(t_{i+1}) + \frac{1}{2}f(t_{i+2})$$

$$a_2 = f(t_{i-1}) - \frac{5}{2}f(t_i) + 2f(t_{i+1}) - \frac{1}{2}f(t_{i+2})$$

$$a_1 = -\frac{1}{2}f(t_{i-1}) + \frac{1}{2}f(t_{i+2})$$

$$a_0 = f(t_i)$$

and $\{(f(t_{i-1}), t_{i-1}), (f(t_i), t_i), (f(t_{i+1}), t_{i+1}), (f(t_{i+2}), t_{i+2})\}$ represent the 4 point neighborhood of the ith discrete point on the sketch.

Appendix 2

Curvature is well defined in the continuous domain, however, estimating curvature in the discrete domain is more difficult because of the sampling process.

As discussed in Chap. 3, curvature is defined (see [10]) as the magnitude of the derivative unit tangent vector with respect to arc length, s (in the continuous domain). That is,

$$\kappa(s) = \left| \frac{\partial^2 \alpha^*}{\partial s^2} \right|, \tag{3.14}$$

assuming the curve is unit speed. However, if the curve is not unit speed then the curvature of any plane curve is

$$\kappa(t) = \frac{\frac{\partial \alpha^*}{\partial x}(t) \frac{\partial^2 \alpha^*}{\partial y^2}(t) - \frac{\partial^2 \alpha^*}{\partial x^2}(t) \frac{\partial \alpha^*}{\partial y}(t)}{\left(\left(\frac{\partial \alpha^*}{\partial x}(t) \right) + \left(\frac{\partial \alpha^*}{\partial y}(t) \right) \right)^{\frac{3}{2}}} \tag{3.15}$$

where t denotes time.

In either case, the curves are assumed to be continuous and twice differentiable. Both of which are only approximately true with discretely sampled sketches (i.e. discrete samples are assumed to be connected using by some continuous segment except for endpoints, and derivatives are approximate).

In practice, when working with discrete curves, curvature must be estimated. The general rule is that curvature at a point is the reciprocal of the radius of the osculating circle—the circle that best approximates the curve around that point (Fig. 3.6). Determining the osculating circle at point q_i is performed (as in [5]) using the following algorithm (depicted in Fig. 3.7):

1. Determine k_b (k_f)—the length of the longest backward (forward) digital straight segment (DSS) from the point q_i.

Fig. 3.6 Osculating *circle*
with radius r

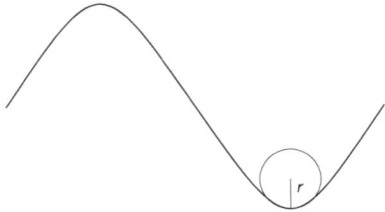

2. Find the bisecting lines ℓ_b and ℓ_f of the line segments from q_{i-k_b} to q_i and from
   q_i to q_{i+k_f} respectively.
3. Compute the center of the osculating circle, c as the intersection of ℓ_b and ℓ_f.
4. Compute the radius of the osculating circle as the Euclidean distance between c
   and the point q_i.
5. Compute curvature as $\frac{1}{r}$.

The radius of the osculating circle is computed, like [4] (cited in [9]), as

$$r = \frac{s_1 s_2 s_3}{\sqrt{(s_1 + s_2 + s_3)(-s_1 + s_2 + s_3)(s_1 - s_2 + s_3)(s_1 + s_2 - s_3)}}$$

where $s_1 = \|q_i - q_{i-k_b}\|$, $s_2 = \|q_i - q_{i+k_f}\|$, and $s_3 = \|q_{i-k_b} - q_{i+k_f}\|$. This algorithm
is illustrated in Fig. 3.7.

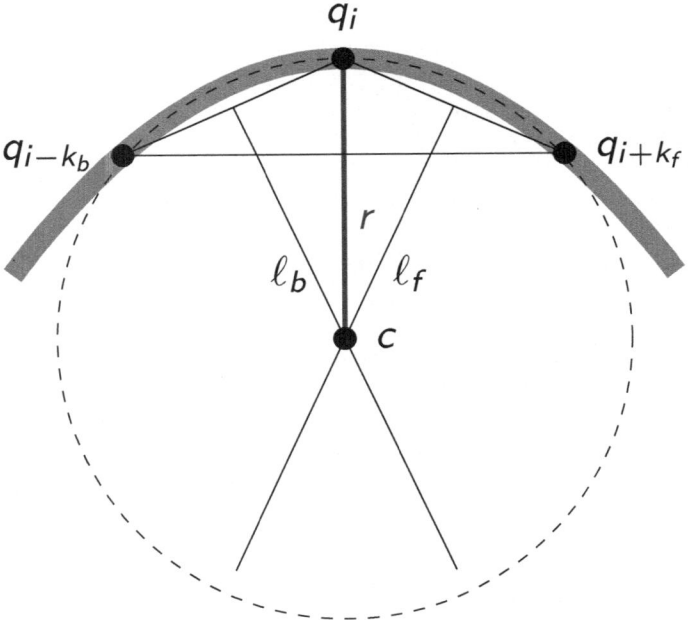

Fig. 3.7 Estimation of the osculating *circle* at q_i. The radius r is shown as the *line* between the
circumcenter c and the *point* q_i

References

1. D. Ballard. Generalizing the Hough Transform to Detect Arbitrary Shapes. *Pattern Recognition*, 13(2):111–122, 1981.
2. R. Bellman. *Dynamic Programming*. Princton University Press, 1957.
3. R. O. Duda, P. E. Hart, and D. G. Stork. *Pattern Classification*. John Wiley & Sons, 2nd edition, 2001.
4. J. Harris and H. Stocker. *Handbook of mathematics and computational science*. Springer-Verlag, 1998.
5. S. Hermann and R. Klette. A comparative study on 2D curvature estimators. *Proc. of the Int'l. Conf. on Computing: Theory and Applications*, pages 584–589, 2007.
6. D. G. Kendall. The diffusion of shape. *Advances in Applied Probability*, 9(3):428–430, 1977.
7. D. G. Kendall, D. Barden, T. K. Carne, and H. Le. *Shape and shape theory*. John Wiley & Sons, 1999.
8. K. Krish, S. Heinrich, W. E. Snyder, H. Cakir, and S. Khorram. Global registration of overlapping images using accumulative image features. *Pattern Recognition Letters*, 31:112–118, 2010.
9. T. P. Nguyen and I. Debled-Rennesson. Curvature estimation in noisy curves. *Proc. of the 12th Int'l Conf. on Computer Analysis of Images and Patterns*, pages 474–481, 2007.
10. J. Opera. *Differential geometry and its applications*, chapter 1, page 17. Pearson Education, 2007.
11. W. E. Snyder. A strategy for shape recognition. In A. Srivastava, editor, *Workshop on Challenges and Opportunities in Image Understanding*, College Park, MD, Jan. 2007.
12. F. Zhou and F. De la Torre. Canonical time warping for alignment of human behavior. *Advances in Neural Information Processing Systems 22*, pages 2286–2294, 2009.
13. F. Zhou and F. De la Torre. Generalized time warping for multi-modal alignment of human motion. *IEEE Conf. on Computer Vision and Pattern Recognition*, pages 1282–1289, June 2012.

Chapter 4
Efficiency, Uniqueness, and Robustness

Abstract There are (at least) three primary considerations when designing a sketch-based authentication system: computational complexity, security, and tolerance. In this chapter, using the generalized Simple K-Space (SKS) approach, the efficiency of model construction is studied. There are two algorithmic implementations to construct this model: the direct/forward approach (or primal algorithm) or the indirect/backward (or dual algorithm). The efficiency of constructing the SKS model is important because the model is most definitely the computational bottleneck of this method. Here, the dual algorithm is shown to enable the use of a model approximation that significantly improves the efficiency for computing the high dimensional model representation. Also, the tradeoff between security and usability is analyzed using SKS. In particular, it is demonstrated that as smoothing parameters of the SKS model asymptotically approach zero, the model is unique and provides "perfect security." However, we also demonstrate the model is generally not unique, but more robust, when a sufficient amount of smoothing occurs over the model. Therefore, SKS is shown to explicitly provide fine-tuned controllability of the security/usability tradeoff.

Keywords Efficiency · Uniqueness · Robustness · Tolerance · Security · Usability

In this chapter, a theoretical analysis on the computational efficiency, uniqueness, and robustness of the SKS-based approach from Chap. 3 is provided. Here, we explicitly claim that the generalized SKS model, despite (essentially) being a multivariate probability density function, is tractable, locally distinct, and tolerant. Additionally, we demonstrate the relationship between the uniqueness and robustness properties, which directly mirror the tradeoff between security and usability.

Later (Chap. 6), specific implementation and experimental results are provided, some of which support the theoretical arguments supplied here.

4.1 Efficiency

In this section, we discuss both direct (i.e. primal) and indirect (i.e. dual) algorithmic implementations for constructing the generalized SKS model. The dual algorithm is shown to produce a model which is sufficiently representative of the model produced

© The Author(s) 2014
B. S. Riggan et al., *Fundamentals of Sketch-Based Passwords*,
SpringerBriefs in Computer Science, DOI 10.1007/978-3-319-13629-5_4

by the primal algorithm. Moreover, the dual is shown to enable an approximation technique to eliminate wasteful computational cycles, allowing a more efficient model construction.

The primal and dual algorithms are described below.

4.1.1 Primal

The primal (Algorithm 4.1) is the direct approach for computing the SKS model in Eq. 3.9. The first step before constructing the model is initializing the model values for all sample points in the feature space to zero. Then, for each sample point, $\mathbf{v} \in \mathcal{F}$, calculate the corresponding model value, $m(\mathbf{v})$, by performing the summation (given by Eq. 3.9) over the entire sketch.

Algorithm 4.1 Primal

```
Initialize: m(v) = 0   ∀v
for v ∈ F {
   for i = 1...n {
       m(v) = m(v) + exp(-½(v - vᵢ)ᵀΣ⁻¹(v - vᵢ))
   }
}
```

$$\text{Initialize: } m(\mathbf{v}) = 0 \quad \forall \mathbf{v}$$
$$\text{for } \mathbf{v} \in \mathcal{F} \; \{$$
$$\quad \text{for } i = 1 \ldots n \; \{$$
$$\qquad m(\mathbf{v}) = m(\mathbf{v}) + \exp\left(-\tfrac{1}{2}(\mathbf{v} - \mathbf{v}_i)^T \Sigma^{-1}(\mathbf{v} - \mathbf{v}_i)\right)$$
$$\quad \}$$
$$\}$$

The primal algorithm, while correct, is terribly inefficient.

It is important to recognize the size of the feature space, denoted as $\text{Card}(\mathcal{F})$, is much larger than the number sketch samples, i.e. $\text{Card}(\mathcal{F}) \gg n$. Therefore, we can show that a significant portion of the model remains null, meaning that

$$\frac{\text{Null}(\mathcal{F})}{\text{Card}(\mathcal{F})} = \frac{\text{Card}(\{\mathbf{v}|m(\mathbf{v}) = 0 \quad \forall \mathbf{v} \in \mathcal{F}\})}{\text{Card}(\mathcal{F})} > r$$

Let $\Sigma \to \mathbf{0}$ denote that the elements of Σ tend toward zero[1], which indicates no smoothing of the model. Then,

$$\lim_{\Sigma \to \mathbf{0}} m(\mathbf{v}) = \sum_{i=0}^{n} \lim_{\Sigma \to \mathbf{0}} \exp\left(-\frac{1}{2}(\mathbf{v} - \mathbf{v}_i)^T \Sigma^{-1}(\mathbf{v} - \mathbf{v}_i)\right)$$
$$= \sum_{i=1}^{n} \delta(\mathbf{v} - \mathbf{v}_i)$$

---

[1] Since Σ is a positive definite matrix, not all elements can be equal to zero. Therefore, the elements tend toward zero while maintaining the positive definite property of the matrix. One way for this to occur is by letting a asymptotically approach 0 and $\Sigma = a\Sigma_0$ for some initial positive definite matrix Σ_0.

where

$$\delta(\mathbf{u}) = \begin{cases} 1 & \mathbf{u} = \mathbf{0} \\ 0 & else \end{cases}$$

Therefore, if the model in the limit as $\Sigma \to \mathbf{0}$ is constructed, then the number of non-zero points bounded between 1 and n. For the upper boundary, the features for each sample along the sketch are distinct, meaning $\mathbf{v}_i \neq \mathbf{v}_j$ for all $i \neq j$. For the lower bound, $\mathbf{v}_i = \mathbf{v}_j \quad \forall i, j$, meaning that a particular set of features is produced by all points along the sketch[2].

Since the upper bound on the number of non-zero points over the model is n, $\text{Null}(\mathcal{F}) \geq \text{Card}(\mathcal{F}) - n$ (in the limit). Therefore,

$$\frac{\text{Null}(\mathcal{F})}{\text{Card}(\mathcal{F})} \geq \frac{\text{Card}(\mathcal{F}) - n}{\text{Card}(\mathcal{F})} \approx 1$$

On the other hand, in the limit as $\Sigma \to \infty$ (indicating uniform smoothing over the entire model, i.e. infinite bandwidth), all points in the model are non-zero, or $\text{Null}(\mathcal{F}) = 0$. Therefore,

$$\frac{\text{Null}(\mathcal{F})}{\text{Card}(\mathcal{F})} \geq \frac{0}{\text{Card}(\mathcal{F})} = 0$$

Note that in most cases uniform smoothing is atypical. Essentially, uniform smoothing saturates the model estimate and eliminates any useful information about the sketch. Therefore, typical smoothing will ensure that $\text{Null}(\mathcal{F}) > 0$, and thus

$$\frac{\text{Null}(\mathcal{F})}{\text{Card}(\mathcal{F})} > r,$$

where $0 < r \leq 1$. If the value of r is sufficiently large, e.g. greater than 0.5, then the primal algorithm unnecessarily loops over the sketch many time for points that will ultimately result in $m(\mathbf{v}) = 0$. The dual algorithm uses an approximation in order to reduce the number of wasted CPU cycles, which improves efficiency of the SKS algorithm in general.

4.1.2 Dual

The dual algorithm (Algorithm 4.2) is an alternative approach for constructing the model (Eq. 3.9). Similar to the primal, the dual first initializes the model. Then, for

---

[2] In the case of a 2D model, consider a perfect circle. All points have the same distance and curvature pairs (assuming the reference is the center of the circle).

each sample point along the sketch, the model is updated incrementally for each point in the feature space.

Algorithm 4.2 Dual

```
Initialize: m(v) = 0  ∀v
for i = 1...n {
    for v ∈ F {
        m(v) = m(v) + exp(-½(v - vᵢ)ᵀ Σ⁻¹(v - vᵢ))
    }
}
```

Note that the primal and dual algorithms construct identical models and have precisely the same computational complexity: $O(n\mathrm{Card}(\mathcal{F}))$. This is because the only difference is the order of the *for loops*.

The dual (Algorithm 4.2) enables an efficient way to approximate the generalized SKS model. Since every point over the model is updated by a factor:

$$\exp\left(-\frac{1}{2}(\mathbf{v} - \mathbf{v}_i)^T \Sigma^{-1}(\mathbf{v} - \mathbf{v}_i)\right)$$

which represents a multivariate Gaussian centered at $\mathbf{v}_i$ in the feature space, only points in the feature space that lie within a reasonable local neighborhood (e.g. defined by the 2Σ or 3Σ hyperellipsoid) about $\mathbf{v}_i$. Thus, the computational complexity of computing the model is significantly reduced. Using this type of local neighborhood, we can show that the dual algorithm scales linearly with the number of sample points along the sketch (Remark 4.1.2).

> *Remark 4.1* The computational complexity for constructing the model is $O(n)$, assuming a fixed neighborhood size.

Proof For each $\mathbf{v}_i$, where $i = 1\ldots n$, along the sketch, the model is updated for every feature point inside the corresponding local neighborhood, N_i. Thus, in general, the computational complexity is $O\left(\sum_{i=1}^{n} |N_i|\right)$, where $|N_i|$ denote the size of the local neighborhood. Assuming that the neighborhood size is constant: $N_i = N$ for $i = 1 \ldots n$, then the computational complexity reduces to

$$O\left(\sum_{i=1}^{n} N\right) = O(nN)$$

$$= O(n).$$

Therefore, the computational complexity scales linearly with the number of sample points along the sketch.   □

4.2   Uniqueness

Next, the property of uniqueness[3] for the generalized SKS model is discussed. The model in Eq. 3.9 can be shown to be unique in the limit as $\Sigma \rightarrow \mathbf{0}$. The uniqueness property is primarily motivated by the original SKS formulation (Eq. 3.7), but uniqueness also extends to the generalized SKS model.

Consider the mapping $\psi : \mathbb{R}^{d \times n} \rightarrow \mathbb{R}^{\mathrm{Card}(\mathcal{F})}$, which maps an element from the "space of sketches" to the "space of model," denoted by $\mathcal{S}$ and $\mathcal{M}$ respectively. Note the distinction between $m(\mathbf{v})$, which maps an element, $\mathbf{v} \in \mathcal{F}$, to a scalar value, and ψ mapping a sketch to some hyper-surface defined by $(\mathbf{v}, m(\mathbf{v})) \ \forall \mathbf{v} \in \mathcal{F}$.

Here, we prove that the mapping ψ is an injective function in the limit (Theorem 4.1), which implies a sense of "perfect security." The term perfect security refers to the fact a sketch must be perfectly replicated due to no smoothing of the model.

> **Theorem 4.1**   *In the limit as* $\Sigma \rightarrow \mathbf{0}$, *two generalized SKS models* $\psi(^{1}\mathbf{X})$ *and* $\psi(^{2}\mathbf{X})$ *of two sketches,* $^{1}\mathbf{X}$ *and* $^{2}\mathbf{X}$, *are equal if and only if* $^{1}\mathbf{X}$ *and* $^{2}\mathbf{X}$ *are related by some isometry (e.g. translation, rotation, or rotation).*

In order to prove Theorem 4.1, a necessary and sufficient condition is that the features used to construct the model are invariant to any isometry. In the 2D case, consider the distance-curvature feature pair; both are invariant to translations, rotations, and reflections. Thus, the model is invariant to isometries too. As stated previously, in the generalized model, the features must move with sketch in order to construct an invariant model (which is the goal of the SKS philosophy). Since we consider a distance and a vector of sketch properties (e.g. curvature, direction, order, pressure, etc.). Therefore, two sketches are related by an isometry if and only if the corresponding set of features, $^{1}\mathbf{V}$ and $^{2}\mathbf{V}$ respectively, are equal[4].

Now, we can effectively prove Theorem 4.1.

Proof   Assume that $^{1}\mathbf{X}$ and $^{2}\mathbf{X}$ are related by some isometry. From the argument above, this implies that the corresponding set of features for each sketch respectively are equal. Therefore,

$$\lim_{\Sigma \rightarrow \mathbf{0}} {}^{1}m(\mathbf{v}) = \sum_{i=1}^{n} \delta(\mathbf{v} - {}^{1}\mathbf{v}_i)$$

---

[3] Here, uniqueness implies a one-to-one mapping from a class of equivalent sketch-based passwords to models.

[4] Equality, here, means either the ordered or unordered set of features are exactly the same if order is preserved or ignored respectively. If order of the features matters, then model accounts for this order by included order as a feature. If order does not matter, as with the original 2D SKS model, then order is remove d during model construction.

$$= \sum_{i=1}^{n} \delta(\mathbf{v} - {}^{2}\mathbf{v}_{i})$$

$$= \lim_{\Sigma \to 0} {}^{2}m(\mathbf{v})$$

Thus, $\psi({}^{1}\mathbf{X}) = \psi({}^{2}\mathbf{X})$.

Conversely, we want to show that $\psi({}^{1}\mathbf{X}) = \psi({}^{2}\mathbf{X})$ implies that ${}^{1}\mathbf{X}$ and ${}^{2}\mathbf{X}$ are related by some isometry (indicating the sketches are in the same equivalence class). However, if the contrapositive: ${}^{1}\mathbf{X}$ and ${}^{2}\mathbf{X}$ are *not* related by an isometry implies $\psi({}^{1}\mathbf{X}) \neq \psi({}^{2}\mathbf{X})$ is true, then the original statement itself is also true.

So, assuming that ${}^{1}\mathbf{X}$ and ${}^{2}\mathbf{X}$ are not related by an isometry, then we know that ${}^{1}\mathbf{V} \neq {}^{2}\mathbf{V}$. Therefore, $\exists i_0$ such that $\mathbf{v}_0 = {}^{1}\mathbf{v}_{i_0} \neq {}^{2}\mathbf{v}_j$ for all $j = 1 \ldots n$. Then, it follows that:

$$\lim_{\Sigma \to 0} {}^{1}m(\mathbf{v}_0) = \sum_{i=1}^{n} \delta(\mathbf{v}_0 - {}^{1}\mathbf{v}_i) \geq 1$$

and

$$\lim_{\Sigma \to 0} {}^{2}m(\mathbf{v}_0) = \sum_{i=1}^{n} \delta(\mathbf{v}_0 - 2\mathbf{v}_i) = 0.$$

Thus, $\psi({}^{1}\mathbf{X}) \neq \psi({}^{2}\mathbf{X})$. $\square$

This concept of uniqueness implies that a sketch must be perfectly replicated (up to a rigid transformation) in order to sufficiently match because there is absolutely no smoothing in the model. As mentioned previously, this is called "perfect security," but there exists a "perfect security paradox." The paradox is that in terms of model smoothing, no amount of tolerance is allowed. However, in terms of information security, the fact that ψ is injective function implies that the mapping is invertible. Therefore, knowing the model (or template) provides all the necessary information about the sketch-based password[5]. Thus, it is preferable to relax the no smoothing constraint.

This concept of uniqueness does not theoretically hold for arbitrary Σ (e.g. uniform, infinite bandwidth smoothing). Due to the paradox, we intentionally prefer that the model is not theoretically injective, for sake of better security and more tolerance. Intuitively, we are claiming that, in general, uniqueness is only a local property of the mapping, ψ.

4.3 Robustness

In this section, the focus is more toward the tolerance built directly into the model. This tolerance, as we demonstrate, implies a sense of usability.

---

[5] The subject of this text does not focus on template security. That is an entirely different subject

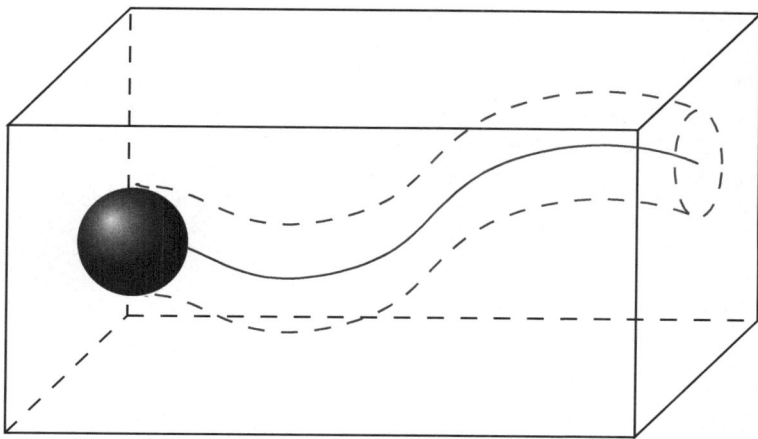

Fig. 4.1 The central path represents the path, defined over the features space, which maximizes the peak in the accumulator. For every point along this path, there exists a point-wise tolerance region (which depends on Σ). Propagating the tolerance region down the central path, produces a "tube" that defines an overall tolerance region for the give model. Conceptually, every path that lies within the model's overall tolerance region corresponds to some sketch that is sufficiently consistent with that model

Given a model, $m(\mathbf{v})$, there exists some ideal path (i.e. a set of points for the discrete case) over the feature space that maximizes the peak in the accumulator (Eq. 3.10). This is depicted in Fig. 4.1. In principle, this path is defined by the sketch, $\mathbf{X}$, that constructed the model. Therefore, if Σ is relaxed to allow some "small" amount of smoothing, then there exists a small "band" or "tube" around the ideal path, which defines some allowable deviation that result in a near optimal accumulator peak. Therefore, the smoothing parameters defined in the matrix Σ directly control the amount tolerance built into the model. This tolerance makes the system more usable.

The fact that reduced smoothing implies a more unique model and less usability (and the opposite effects for increased smoothing) demonstrates that the Σ directly controls the tradeoff between security and usability.

While this tradeoff also exists for a DTW-based system, the only parameter that effects the tradeoff is the decision threshold. However, with an SKS approach, the smoothing parameters provide more degrees of freedom, and thus a fine-tuned control of the the security/usability tradeoff.

4.4 Key Points

The primary results from this chapter include:

1. The dual algorithm enable an efficient computation of the generalized SKS model using a local neighborhood approximation.

2. The computation complexity of constructing the model scales linearly with the the number of sketch samples (assuming fix neighborhood size).
3. In the limit as $\Sigma \to \mathbf{0}$, the generalized SKS models are unique.
4. Generally, uniqueness is only a local property, not a global one.
5. SKS explicitly provide parameters for a robust model.
6. Uniqueness implies security, and robustness implies tolerance.
7. Σ provides fine-tuned controllability of the security/usability tradeoff.

Chapter 5
Human-Computer Interaction

Abstract The main objective of this chapter is to summarize the authors' recent work which studied the human-computer interaction for sketch-based passwords. However, before discussing the previous results, the features used specifically for implementation of SKS are discussed, and an overview of the database used for the HCI study (and some experiments and results in the subsequent chapter) is provided. The features used for the application of sketch-based passwords incorporates four fundamental properties: (1) shape, (2) direction, (3) order, and (4) pressure, which comprise a local 5D feature descriptor at every sketch sample point. The database used for this HCI study was constructed by the authors in (Riggan et al., A human factors study of graphical passwords using biometrics. Proc. of the 36th German Conf. on Pattern Recognition, 2014). This database considers a sufficiently large and complete set of users and many variations of sketch-based passwords. The previous HCI is useful to understand the connection between human perception and certain similarity measures, specifically for sketch-based authentication.

Keywords BioSketch database · HCI · Variability analysis

In this chapter, previous human-computer interaction (HCI) study [6] for sketch-based authentication systems is summarized. The analysis of any HCI may be rather difficult because of the *human in the loop*. In the case of sketch-based passwords, recognition accuracy depends on the genuine users ability to replicate his/her sketch.

What exactly makes HCI analysis more difficult than other analyses? In most recognition problems, e.g. face recognition or fingerprint recognition, the ground truth is well defined, meaning from training/testing sets the identities associated with different faces or fingerprints are known. While there are some known variations (e.g. occlusion, pose, lighting) that may cause recognition failure, a person cannot intentionally change his/her face to the point that it appears to belong to another person (from a human visual system level of recognition). However, the *ground truth problem* for sketch-based authentication is that the ground truth is not as well defined as other recognition tasks, such as face and fingerprint recognition. While the person who drew the sketch is known, the quality of the sketch provided is uncertain. If a user is supposed to draw a "smiley face," it is more difficult to guarantee that the sketch is not intentionally corrupted without introducing some amount of bias. Allowing such critical errors into a dataset has adverse effects on recognition performance. Limiting the sketch to only the "best" biases the results. Therefore, the goal is to include only

B. S. Riggan et al., *Fundamentals of Sketch-Based Passwords,*
SpringerBriefs in Computer Science, DOI 10.1007/978-3-319-13629-5_5

"natural" variations of sketches, but the line between natural and unnatural variation is extremely blurred.

The following sections discuss: (1) features used in testing, (2) the BioSketch database, (3) similarity measures used for the HCI analysis, and (4) the HCI analysis results.

5.1 Features

Before discussing the HCI analysis or the performance analysis in Chap. 6, a discussion of specific sketch features is necessary.

There are several properties that are important for representing a sketch-based password:

1. shape
2. dynamics
3. order
4. biometrics

The shape features used in testing the generalized SKS framework are the same features: distance and curvature (Sect. 3.2.2.1). In the application of sketch-based passwords, the shape is not the only component that should be captured. For example, two collections of points with identical spatial locations, but have different dynamics and/or ordering, are considered to have the same shape. Therefore, these two *distinctive* passwords (represented by the collection of points) are considered similar if only shape features are used.

Example dynamic features include: velocity, acceleration, tangential acceleration, etc. In the this brief, only the directional component of the local velocity vector is used. Experimentally, we found that the magnitude component of velocity did not have critical impact on performance.

The order component is a necessary property for sketch-based passwords because the sampling ordering should be preserved. As mentioned earlier in Chap. 3, for shape recognition applications the parameterization can be integrated out. However, for recognition of sketch-based passwords the parameterization should be explicitly incorporated into the model. This is achieved by using arc length as a feature.

Lastly, biometric properties for sketch-based passwords are necessary for improving the security of sketch-based authentication system. In particular, the biometric property used in this work is *pressure*. Therefore, the feature space is a 5D, where the respective dimension are: distance (ρ), curvature (κ), direction (θ), order (s), and pressure (b).

Next, the database that used for the HCI analysis is briefly discussed.

5.2 BioSketch Database

The ground truth problem is common among HCI applications, and is usually handled through controlled studies. Therefore, the BioSketch database [5], which was constructed in controlled environment with limited (if any) biasing effects, is used to provide a controlled variability analysis.

The BioSketch database measures the essential properties for every sketch sample point:

- position: x-y coordinates (defined by the screen's active drawing area)
- pressure: denoted as b
- time: denoted at t (in milliseconds)

Other local features may be derived directly from these properties, e.g. relative distances, curvature, velocity, acceleration, etc. Therefore, the BioSketch database is designed to be more general than the DooDB database [3, 4]. The BioSketch database is constructed from a total of 35 genuine users (plus additional 15 skilled forgers) who provided a total of 80 sketches each, which are composed of 40 sketches drawn with increased stability (drawn at two significantly different times) and 40 sketches drawn with decreased stability (drawn at two significantly different times). Example sketch-based passwords from this database are shown in Fig. 5.1.

There are multiple restrictions used to control the sketches collected, including:

1. stability
2. time lapse (within and between sessions)
3. drawing complexity
4. qualitative reproducibility/familiarity

First, using the same sketch-based password, users provide instances with the tablet laying flat on the surfaces of desk/table and with the tablet firmly held in their hands. This allows us to determine how different stability cases affect the variability. Second, the users provide instances of a sketch-based password during two separate sessions, which are separated by a sufficient amount of time (e.g. 7–10 days). This demonstrates the effects from a user having to remember his/her sketch-based password. Next, drawings are somewhat limited so that a fair comparison can be made. If there were no limitations on drawing complexity, then as user preference would probably choose simple and insecure drawings that are easily replicated (e.g. a circle or a line). Therefore, the drawings are restricted as to: (1) consist of a single uninterrupted stroke, (2) consist of more than a single line segment or circle, and (3) be less complex than a signature. The purpose of these constraints is to have a collection of sketches with similar complexities[1]. Finally, the sketches were required to be relatively reproducible to the respective users. While this is only a qualitative restriction,

---

[1] The term complexity, here, refers to the complexity of the drawing itself. There are many possible definition for complexity of a drawing, such as the polynomial order of an appropriate regression model or the number of self-intersections.

Fig. 5.1 Example sketches as part of the BioSketch database [5]

its important cannot be understated. The goal in reproducibility is to ensure that users have some sense familiarity with their own sketch-based password.

For complete details on the BioSketch database refer to [5].

5.3 Similarity Measures

The objective of providing a variability analysis is to better understand the HCI process for sketch-based passwords. Ideally, this analysis should be performed irrespective of any particular method. However, the problem without explicitly knowing the ground truth makes this difficult. Therefore, two measures are considered (as in [5]) for comparison: the Fréchet distance and SKS.

The *Fréchet distance* [1, 2] is used for measuring the dissimilarity between parameterized curves, or in this case sketches. This distance is commonly described using the analogy of person walking a dog with a leash. The Fréchet distance represents the shortest leash required when the person walks forward along a designated path at some speed, and the dog walks forward along another path at another speed. The

Fréchet distance is defined in Eq. 5.1.

$$D_{Fréchet}\left({}^1\mathbf{X}, {}^2\mathbf{X}\right) = \inf_{f,g} \max_i \left\| f\left({}^1\mathbf{v}_i\right) - g\left({}^2\mathbf{v}_i\right) \right\| \tag{5.1}$$

f and g represent monotonic functions, which are used to reparameterize the sketches ${}^1\mathbf{X}$ and ${}^2\mathbf{X}$ respectively.

The generalized SKS (see Chap. 3) is a method that measures similarity by building a probabilistic-like model (Eq. 3.9) and then accumulates (Eq. 3.10) local consistencies between an unknown and the model. SKS may be reformulated by combining Eqs. 3.9 and 3.10, resulting in:

$$S\left({}^1\mathbf{X}, {}^2\mathbf{X}\right) = \max_{\hat{\mathbf{x}}} \sum_{i,j=1}^n \exp\left(-\frac{1}{2}\left({}^2\mathbf{v}_i(\hat{\mathbf{x}}) - {}^1\mathbf{v}_j\right)^T \Sigma^{-1} \left({}^2\mathbf{v}_i(\hat{\mathbf{x}}) - {}^1\mathbf{v}_j\right)\right) \tag{5.2}$$

$$= \max_{\hat{\mathbf{x}}} \sum_{i,j=1}^n \exp\left(-\frac{1}{2}\left(\begin{bmatrix} \|{}^2\mathbf{x}_i - \hat{\mathbf{x}}\| \\ {}^2\kappa_i^* \end{bmatrix} - \begin{bmatrix} {}^1\rho_j \\ {}^1\kappa_j^* \end{bmatrix}\right)^T\right.$$

$$\left.\Sigma^{-1}\left(\begin{bmatrix} \|{}^2\mathbf{x}_i - \hat{\mathbf{x}}\| \\ {}^2\kappa_i^* \end{bmatrix} - \begin{bmatrix} {}^1\rho_j \\ {}^1\kappa_j^* \end{bmatrix}\right)\right)$$

Notice that features, ${}^2\mathbf{V}$, (from the test sketch ${}^2\mathbf{X}$) have a dependency on the estimated reference point $\hat{\mathbf{x}}$. Wheras, the features from the model, ${}^1\mathbf{V}$, do not; the reference (in this case) is constant, but arbitrary.

Searching for the optimal reference point for the test sketch provides more flexibility to non-similarity transformations. However, it is important note that if the model and test sketched were to be switched (i.e. ${}^2\mathbf{X}$ becomes the model and ${}^1\mathbf{X}$ the test sketch), then the similarity value is not the same as the one from Eq. 5.2. Thus, in general,

$$S\left({}^1\mathbf{X}, {}^2\mathbf{X}\right) \neq S\left({}^2\mathbf{X}, {}^1\mathbf{X}\right)$$

which means that SKS is not a symmetric similarity measure. However, a symmetric definition may be defined (as in [5]) as in Eq. 5.3.

$$S'\left({}^1\mathbf{X}, {}^2\mathbf{X}\right) = S\left({}^1\mathbf{X}, {}^2\mathbf{X}\right) + S\left({}^2\mathbf{X}, {}^1\mathbf{X}\right) \tag{5.3}$$

which can be shown to be a semi-metric.

While metrics are typically well behaved, the triangle inequality constraint poorly models human recognition. For example, consider the task of image similarity from pixel intensities. The Euclidean distance is a commonly used metric. While it does obey the triangle inequality, due varying noise, lighting, texture, and pose, the Euclidean distance is a poor model for image similarity. On the contrary, a comparison between probability densities (of pixel intensities) does not necessarily obey the triangle inequality, but is a better model for visual similarity. Therefore, a metric is not necessarily a good model for measuring visual similarity.

Semi-metrics adhere to all properties of a metric except for the triangle inequality: non-negativity, identity, and symmetry. Logically, semi-metrics appear to be useful in visual tasks because:

1. two objects may exhibit no similarity, little similarity, or much similarity (i.e. non-negative similarity)
2. two objects have maximum similarity if and only if the objects are identical
3. the measure of similarity between *object A* and *object B* is equal to that between *object B* and *object A*.

In the next section, a variability analysis for sketch-based passwords is performed using the Frechet distance metric (Eq. 5.1) and the SKS-based similarity semi-metric (Eq. 5.3).

5.4 Variability Analysis

In this section, the results from a variability analysis for sketch-based passwords from [5] are summarized. In [5] the inter and intra class variations are analyzed using both Fréchet distance metric and SKS similarity semi-metric. These variations are used qualitatively demonstrate the differences "matching" and "non-matching" sketch-based passwords. The purpose to this HCI analysis is to study the correlation between human perception and similarity metrics, in the context of sketch-based authentication.

The BioSketch database is contains four subsets: D1, H1, D2, H2. The D1 and D2 sets represent sketches drawn with improved stability (i.e. flat on a desk), and the H1 and H2 sets represent those drawn with less stability (i.e. holding the tablet). Then, session 1 sketches (D1 and H1) and session 2 sketches (D2 and H2) are collected on two different days (7–10 days a parts). For each of the sets, the score distributions for genuine sketches, random forgeries, and skilled forgeries are plotted.

The distributions (Fig. 5.2) are used to illustrate the difference between genuine sketches, random forgeries, and skilled forgeries for D1[2]. The genuine scores are computed using $D_{Fréchet} \left({}^1\mathbf{X}, {}^2\mathbf{X} \right)$ and $S' \left({}^1\mathbf{X}, {}^2\mathbf{X} \right)$ respectively, where ${}^1\mathbf{X}$ and ${}^2\mathbf{X}$ are two sketches drawn by the same person[3]. Random forgery scores are also computed using Eqs. 5.1 and 5.3, except that ${}^1\mathbf{X}$ and ${}^2\mathbf{X}$ come from different users. The random forgery test simulates a brute force style attack on a sketch-based authentication system using each measure. Finally, the skilled forgery scores are obtained by comparing a skilled forgery of a each user's sketch-based password. This test simulates

---

[2] Distributions for H1, D2, and H2 are similar the distributions shown here.

[3] For the D1, H1, D2, and H2 histograms, the reference sketches (i.e. used to build model) come from the D1 session and testing is performed on the sketch from the respective session. Note for the D1 session the scores corresponding to identical sketches are removed from the histogram to reduce result bias.

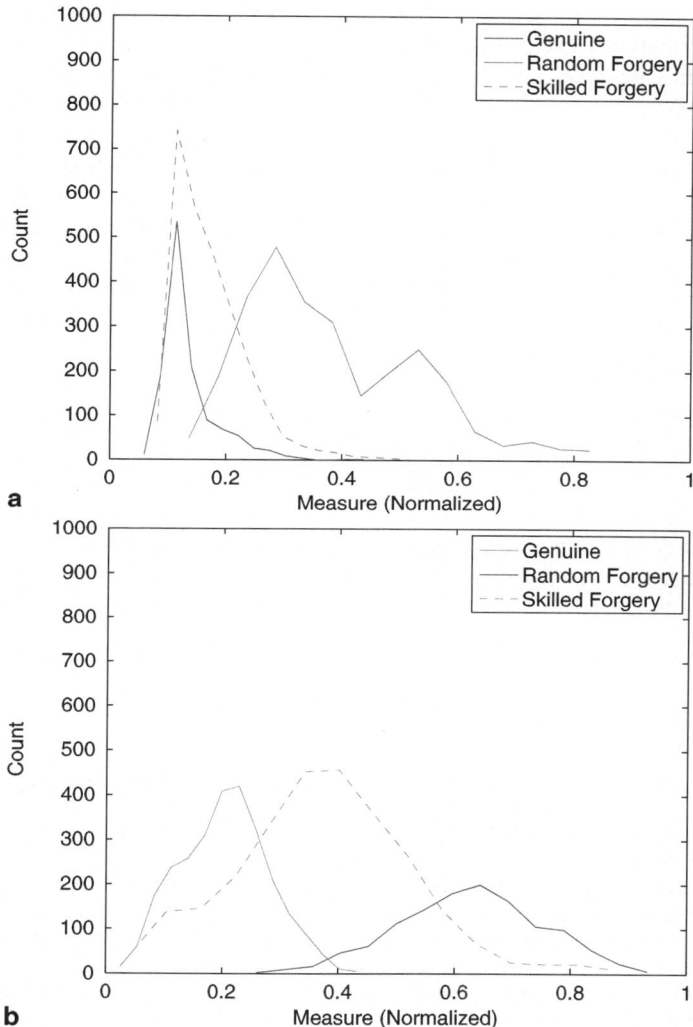

Fig. 5.2 Distributions for the Fréchet distance (**a**) and SKS (**b**). Plots are best viewed in color (refer to online version). (Figures are from [5])

a shoulder surfing attack, where the hacker has some inside information (e.g. what to draw). However, some information (e.g. pressure) is unobservable to the hacker.

In Fig. 5.2, the random forgery overlap, skilled forgery overlap, and distribution attributes (e.g. tails, peaks, and variance) are qualities of interest. The amount of overlap between the genuine scores and random forgery scores is very small for both Fréchet and SKS, and the overlap between the genuine and skilled forgeries is greater. When comparing the Fréchet distance and SKS for D1 (and other sets) it is evident that the amount of overlap is generally less for SKS. Now, consider the attributes of the distributions. The distribution of the genuine scores for exhibits a tail, which indicates the presence of outliers in the data. The peaks in the histograms indicate the most probable scores for genuine sketches and forgeries. Notice that peaks for the genuine sketches and skilled forgeries occur nearly at the same location using the Frechet distance metric, and they are further apart using the SKS similarity semi-metric. Finally, compare the variances of the genuine and forgery histograms: the genuine variance for the Fréchet distance is smaller than that for SKS, which indicates that Fréchet has a more restricted[4] definition of similar than SKS.

5.5 Key Points

The major points from this chapter include:

1. The SKS-based implementation uses: shape, direction, order, and pressure features.
2. The BioSketch database is more general than the DooDB database
3. The HCI study shows shows that SKS has a restricted definition of dissimilar, and the Fréchet distance has a restricted definition of similar.

References

1. P. K. Agarwal, H. K. Avraham, H. Kaplan, and M. Sharir. Computing the discrete freéchet distance in subquadratic time. *Proc. of the 24th Annual ACM-SIAM Symposium on Discrete Algorithms*, pages 156–167, 2013.
2. H. Alt and H. Godau. Computing the fréchet distance between two polygonal curves. *Int'l Journal of Computational Geometry and Applications*, 5(1–2):75–91, 1995.
3. M. Martinez-Diaz, J. Fierrez, C. Martin-Diaz, and J. Ortega-Garcia. DooDB: A Graphical Password Database Containing Doodles and Pseudo-Signatures. *12th Int'l. Conf. on Frontiers in Handwriting Recognition*, pages 339–344, 2010.
4. M. Martinez-Diaz, J. Fierrez, and J. Galbally. The DooDB Graphical Password Database: Data Analysis and Benchmark Results. *IEEE Access*, 1:596–605, 2013.
5. B. S. Riggan, W. E. Snyder, X. Wang, and J Feng. A human factors study of graphical passwords using biometrics. *Proc. of the 36th German Conf. on Pattern Recognition*, 2014.
6. B. S. Riggan, W. E. Snyder, X. Wang, and L. K. Norris. A sketch-based authentication system with biometrics: security and usability analysis. *Pattern Recognition (Under Review)*, 2014.

---

[4] SKS may be more robust than the Frechet distance because it has a broad definition of similar and more narrow definition of different.

Chapter 6
Experiments and Results

Abstract In this chapter, a collection of experiments and results are provided. There are two main sections of experiments: those designed to support the theory discussed in Chap. 4, and a sufficiently complete performance analysis. The first set of experiments study the uniqueness and robustness properties of the Simple K-Space approach. First, an experiment designed to demonstrate that any small change in the sketch results in a corresponding change in the model, indicate a local type of uniqueness (in general). Then, in order to study the robustness of SKS, the model is fixed and the test sketch varied in relatively small increments from the sketch that constructed the (constant) model to a completely different sketch. Analysis of the accumulators from this experiment reveals that initially there is strong peak, which diminishes as the test becomes inconsistent with the model. Thus, SKS directly incorporates tolerance into the methodology. The second set of experiments includes testing the performance on synthesized sketch-based password and two databases of hand-drawn sketches (one includes pressure information and the other does not).

Keywords Performance analysis · FAR · FRR · EER

In this chapter, we demonstrate the feasibility and security of our system through experimentation. In order to demonstrate the current level of performance, several experiments are performed using both synthetic and hand-drawn sketches. The purpose of these experiments is two-fold: (1) to support the uniqueness and robustness claims in Chap. 4 and (2) to provide a performance analysis of the proposed password system.

In this brief, as well as many other biometric systems, performance is measured by the false acceptance rate (FAR) versus the false rejection rate (FRR) curve. The FAR is the number of accepted forgeries divided by the total number of forgeries, and the FRR is the number of genuine sketches that are rejected divided by the total number of genuine sketches. In some cases, performance is reported with a single number referred to as the equal error rate (EER), which is the rate where the FAR and FRR are equal.

© The Author(s) 2014
B. S. Riggan et al., *Fundamentals of Sketch-Based Passwords,*
SpringerBriefs in Computer Science, DOI 10.1007/978-3-319-13629-5_6

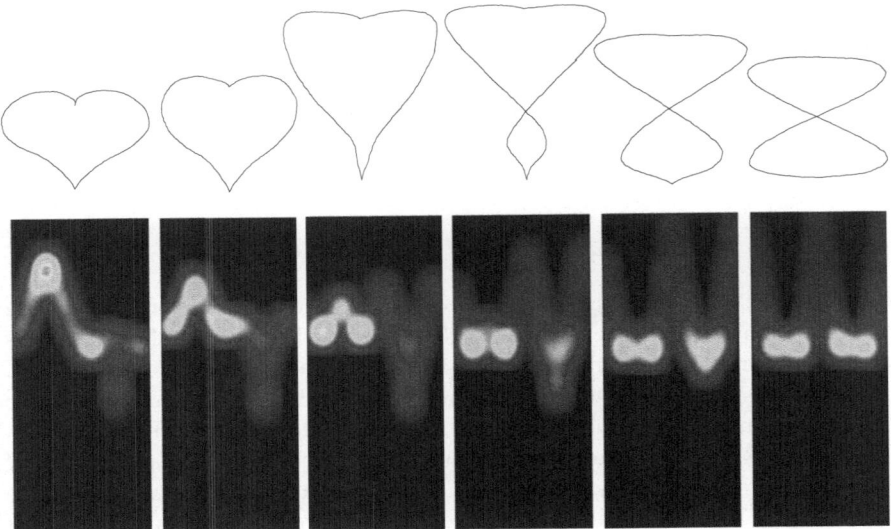

Fig. 6.1 Shows the interpolation between a heart and a figure-8 (*row 1*). Then, the corresponding projections of the models onto the ρ-s plane are shown in *row 2*. Here, we can see that the first two shapes (and models) are more similar than the first and the last. Model images are best shown in color (see online version)

6.1 Uniqueness and Robustness Experiments

6.1.1 Uniqueness

In this set of experiments, we demonstrate that the SKS model is, for all intents and purposes, unique. The idea is to show that a "small" change in the sketch results in a "small" change in the model. These experiments provide some experimental evidence to support Theorem 4.1.

Given any 2 sketches drawn by separate users, 50 intermediate sketches between the 2 are computed. This allows us to consider 50 distinct sketches with corresponding models. Here, the goal is to infer how the model is affected by small changes in the respective sketch. Thus, the relationship between the sketch mean square error (MSE) (between the ith sketch and the 1st sketch) and the model MSE (between the ith model and the 1st model) is considered.

By plotting the model MSE vs. the sketch MSE, we can show that "small" change in the sketch results in a "small" change in the model.

Some examples of this procedure are shown using projections of the higher dimensional models in Fig. 6.1. Notice how every perturbation of the sketch results in a change in the model, which is exactly what we imply when we say that model is (locally) unique. Some example plots of model MSE vs. sketch MSE are shown in Fig. 6.2.

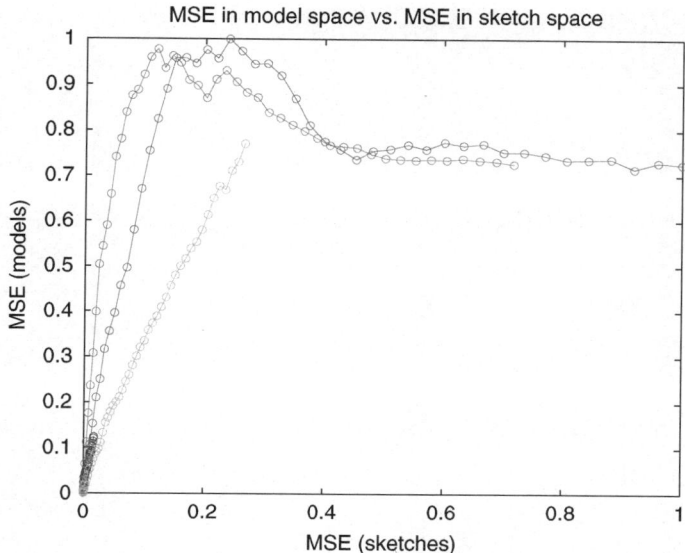

Fig. 6.2 The plot shows how the MSE in the "space of sketches" is reflected in the "space of models" for the interpolation from one sketch to four different sketches. Initially, the MSE is null for both because the sketches and models are identical. However, as the sketches become different, the models also become increasingly different which is reflected in the examples shown here. The exact nature of the curve depends on both starting sketch (model) and ending sketch (model)

6.1.2 Robustness

In the following experiment, we demonstrate the robustness of the accumulative framework. As in the previous section, we use the interpolation between two distinct sketches. While holding the model constant (i.e., let the model be constructed from the first in the interpolated sequence), let the login sketch vary. As the sketch differs, the accumulator peak changes too. Initially, the difference between the accumulator peaks is very little. As the sketch differs more and more, the accumulator peak becomes less distinctive, indicating less similarity between sketches. Therefore, despite small perturbations (from the sketch producing the model) occurring, the accumulator will still exhibit a sufficiently larger peak, indicating a matching sketch. This implies that the matching procedure is intentionally fuzzy, which makes the system more robust.

A sequence of test shapes and the accumulators are shown in Fig. 6.3.

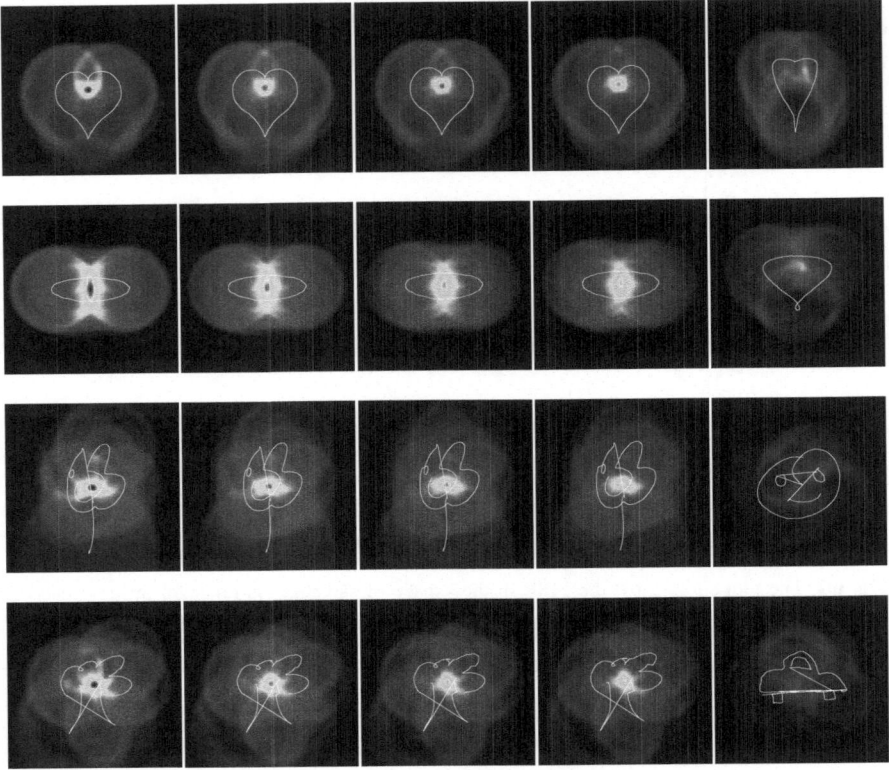

Fig. 6.3 The test sketch is overlaid on the accumulator in order to show how the accumulator changes as the shape is deformed. Notice, how even deformed versions of the same sketch reveal a peak in the accumulator (*columns 1–4*). However, if the sketch is deformed too much the peak is diminished (*column 5*). Refer to the online version for color images

6.2 Performance Analysis

In this section, a sufficiently complete set experiments are provided in order to demonstrate the recognition power for the generalized SKS approach. First, a set of synthetic sketches are used to demonstrate that performance is improved with the addition of specific features (without detrimental effect from the curse of dimensionality). Second, SKS is compared with a DTW-based approach using the DooDB database [1, 2].

6.2.1 Synthetic Sketches

Using a set of parameterized shapes (with normalized scale), an ideal dataset is constructed (Fig. 6.4). From these ideal shapes, random noise is added to the shape. The type of noise we are modeling is jitter, due to the shaking of the hand while drawing a sketch. Using this type of noise, the performance of the algorithm discussed in this paper is computed using four different feature combinations:

1. ρ and κ (Shape features)
2. ρ, κ, and θ (Shape and direction features)
3. ρ, κ, and b (Shape and pressure features)
4. ρ, κ, θ, and b (Shape, direction, and pressure features)

Jitter is modeled by low frequency, additive Gaussian noise. This type of noise is generated by lowpass filtering a sequence of independent Gaussian random variables with zero mean and some variance (σ^2). This low frequency noise is added to the spatial coordinates of the shape, and then the corresponding features are computed using the noisy signal.

A password model is constructed using 3 different noisy instances of a shape, and then tested on a total of 50 noisy shapes (10 of which are the same shape with simulated jitter). This procedure is performed for a total of five different shapes in order to compute FAR and FRR measures. By providing a different set of three sketches (of the same shape) to build each model, we can compute different FAR and FRR measures. Therefore, we repeatedly choose sets of three sketches to build each password model and compute an average FAR and average FRR. In this paper, this is how we will compare each method using different feature combinations.

The performance curves in Fig. 6.5 demonstrate that the generalized SKS method proposed for matching sketch-based passwords presented in the paper improves performance (at least for the synthetic data generated) from the original SKS approach. These results also show that it is much more robust under perturbations due to (low frequency) jitter. In principle, this also indicates the potential robustness to jitter from hand-drawn sketches.

6.2.2 DooDB Database

In this set of experiments, SKS and a DTW-based approach are compared using the DooDB database [1, 2], which contains a set of finger-drawn doodles (or sketches) and pseudo-signatures. For the purposes of comparing our system with a state-of-the-art method, the experiments here are conducted in a similar manner as [1, 2].

The DooDB database contains files which include both spatial and temporal information, which are used for positional, velocity, and acceleration type features. Since their data was collected using a device with a resistive touch screen and without any hardware for detecting pressure, they do not use pressure as a biometric feature.

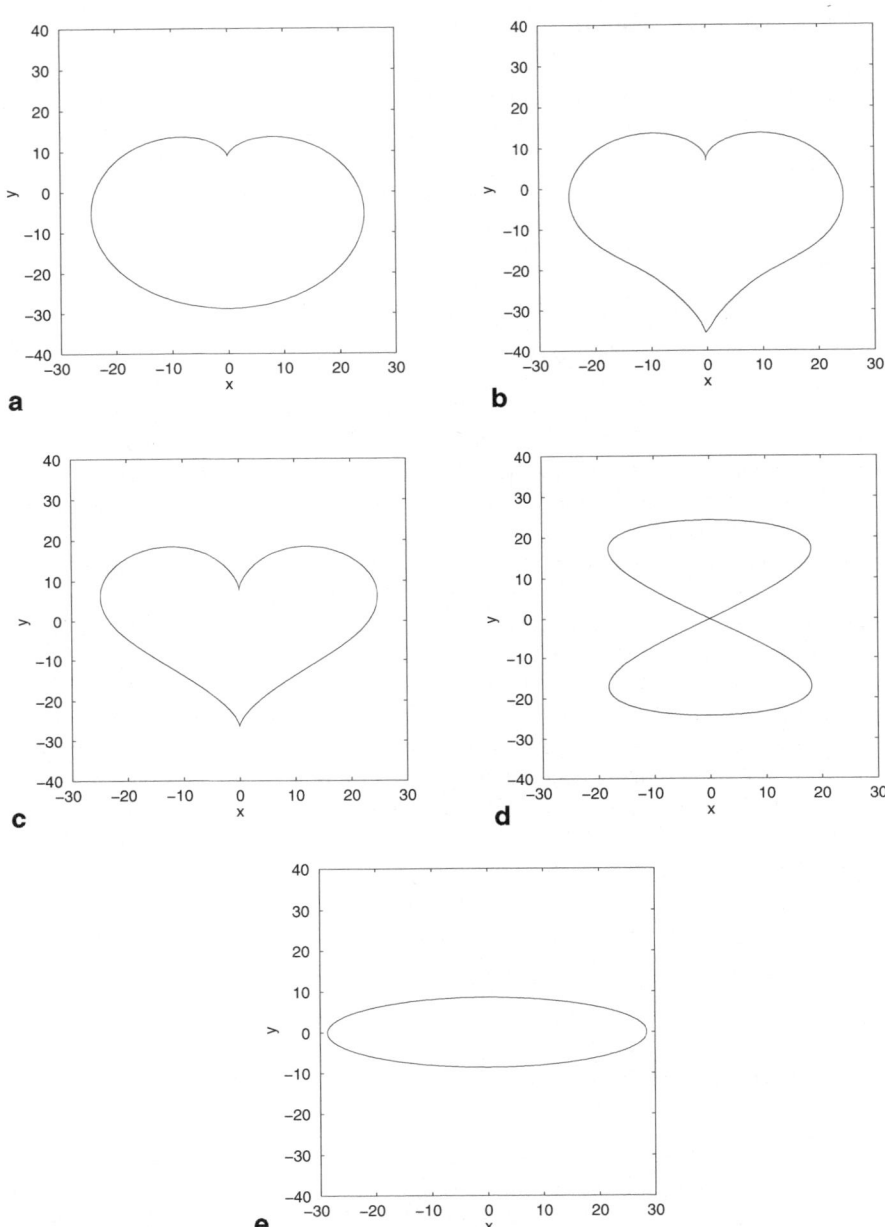

Fig. 6.4 Set of synthetic sketches: **a** heart #1, **b** heart #2, **c** heart #3, **d** figure-8, and **e** ellipse

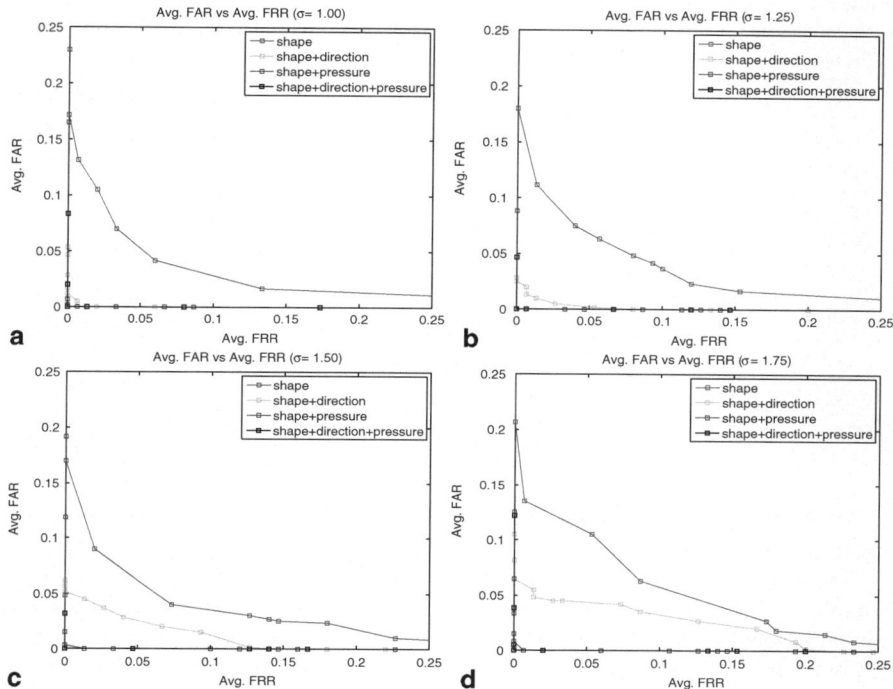

Fig. 6.5 Comparison of average performance curves using different sets of features with varying levels of jitter: **a** $\sigma^2 = 1.00$ pixels, **b** $\sigma^2 = 1.25$ pixels, **c** $\sigma^2 = 1.50$ pixels, and **d** $\sigma^2 = 1.75$ pixels. Refer to the online version for color plots

Therefore, to compare the systems on a level playing field, our system is tested on the DooDB database *without the biometric pressure*. We will demonstrate the advantage of using biometric pressure in Sects. 6.2.3 and 6.2.4.

The performance of our SKS-based method is compared with the method used in [2], which is a Dynamic Time Warping (DTW) based system. They test performance on both doodles (or sketches) and pseudo-signatures, and they report an EER for both random and skilled forgeries (with the expectation that skilled forgeries will have worse performance).

The performance measures used are the random forgery EER (denoted as EER_{rd}) and skilled forgery[1] EER (denoted as EER_{sk}) for both doodles and pseudo-signatures.

The results from [2] and our results are both reported in Table 6.1 for comparison. In [2], three different features sets are used with the

---

[1] A skilled forgery is defined as one in which the forger knows what the sketch looks like as well as its beginning and ending points.

Table 6.1 Performance comparison between DTW and SKS on DooDB database, which included both doodles and pseudo-signatures. The best performance is achieved using the SKS-Bio, which is the approach presented in this paper

Method	Session	Doodles		Pseudo-signatures	
		EER_{rd}	EER_{sk}	EER_{rd}	EER_{sk}
ATVS-Pos	1	2.7	28.0	3.5	28.6
ATVS-Vel	1	3.4	**26.7**	**1.6**	23.9
ATVS-Acc	1	4.5	28.1	2.2	**19.8**
SKS	1	**1.4**	28.0	**1.6**	23.3
ATVS-Pos	2	7.6	36.4	5.0	34.5
ATVS-Vel	2	6.3	**33.9**	**3.8**	29.7
ATVS-Acc	2	7.3	34.1	4.3	**25.0**
SKS	2	**3.8**	35.9	5.2	28.5

DTW method. These features are ATVS-Pos, ATVS-Vel, and ATVS-Acc, which represent the spatial coordinates, velocity, and acceleration features respectively.

The results in Table 6.1 show that even *without biometric pressure* SKS is comparable to (better than in some cases) the DTW method. However, there are some important observations to note. First, SKS appears to perform slightly better than DTW on the doodles, but not on the pseudo-signatures. Recognizing doodles (or sketches) was the objective of our approach, and we have achieved an improved results on the set of doodles. For the pseudo-signature, we still achieve comparable performance to the DTW approach, despite not designing the system with signatures in mind. Second, but probably most significant, is that our system is easily generalized to incorporate features such as biometric pressure as a property of a sketch. Since the DooDB database does not have pressure, we cannot accurately compare the two systems using pressure. However, we believe that biometric pressure significantly improves performance over those systems without it. Finally, the DTW approach tests both velocities and accelerations. In our experiments, we found that the improvement from velocity came more from the direction than the magnitude (or speed). Now, acceleration, which is a second derivative with respect to time, is a very noisy feature. In some cases, acceleration improves performance and in others acceleration worsens it.

Additional results are shown in Fig. 6.6.

6.2.3 BioSketch Database

This section summarizes performance results on the BioSketch database [3] (see Chap. 5).

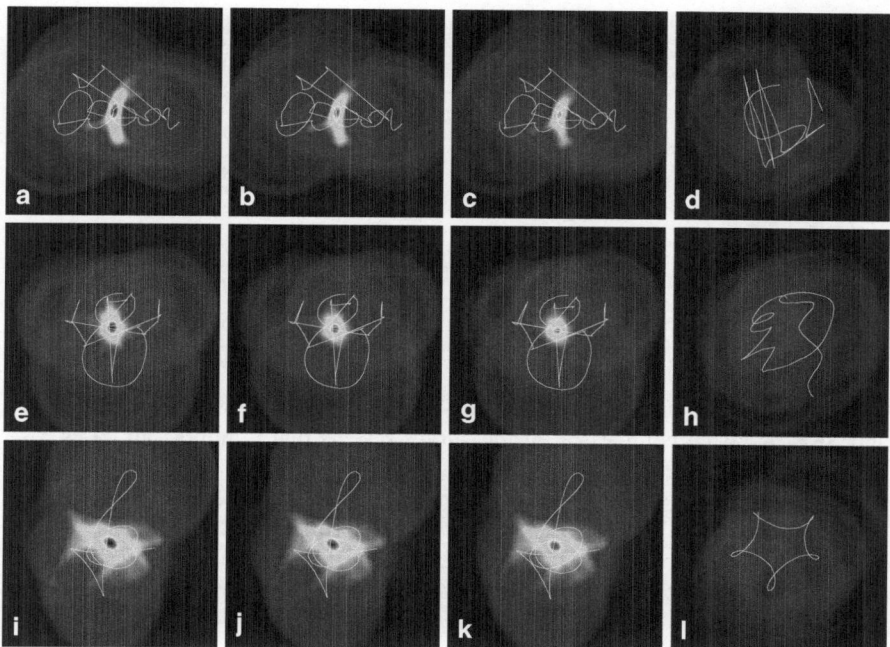

Fig. 6.6 Example matching accumulators with overlaid test sketches are shown in *column (1–3)*. The *last column* shown non-matching accumulators. Refer to the online version for color images

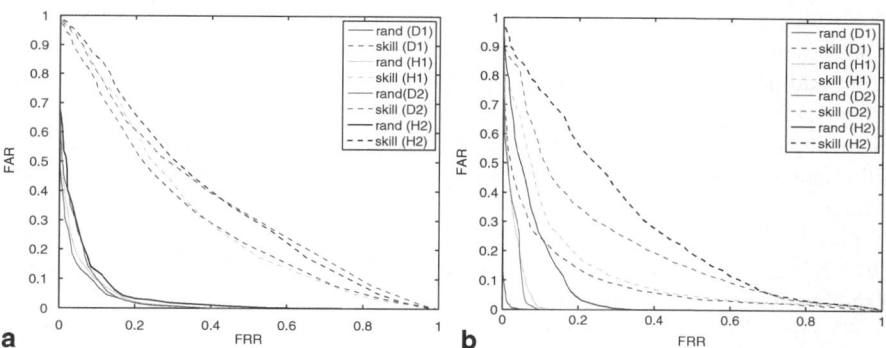

Fig. 6.7 FAR vs. FRR curves using the Fréchet distance and SKS. Plots are best viewed in color (see online version). (Figures are originally from [3])

In most systems, performance is measured by the false acceptance rate (FAR)—percentage of forgeries wrongly considered to be genuine—versus the false rejection rate (FRR)—percentage of genuine sketches considered to be a forgery. Therefore, the performance curves are shown for both Fréchet and SKS methods (Fig. 6.7).

Table 6.2 Summary of EER (%) performances using the Fréchet distance and SKS. (Table is from [3])

Session	Method	EER_{rd}	EER_{sk}
D1	Fréchet	9.05	34.36
	SKS	**1.74**	**16.75**
H1	Fréchet	9.76	34.73
	SKS	**6.85**	**19.10**
D2	Fréchet	9.97	39.55
	SKS	**5.72**	**27.86**
H2	Fréchet	**11.22**	39.96
	SKS	14.57	**34.52**

Notice the differences between the performance curves using the Fréchet distance and SKS. A visual comparison of the curves reveals that in almost all cases SKS outperforms the Fréchet distance.

In order to better compare performance, Table 6.2 shows the random and skilled equal error rates (EERs)—the rate at which FAR is equal to FRR—for each method using the four sets of sketches (D1, H1, D2, H2). The results show as much as a 7 % reduction in EER between the Fréchet distance and SKS using random forgeries and a 17 % reduction for skilled.

6.2.4 Pressure as a Biometric

The following set of experiments aims to demonstrate the potential security benefit from adding biometric pressure to sketch-based password systems. A total of 100 sketches (with pressure information) from 5 different users were obtained using a Samsung Galaxy Note® 10.1. Each of the 5 users provided 10 genuine sketches (i.e. 50 genuine sketches in total), and the remainder of the 100 sketches were skilled forgeries. Similar to the experiments performed on the DooDB database, we build a model using 3–5 example sketches (the first 3–5 sketches provided) and measure the verification performances (in terms of EER_{rd} and EER_{sk}) on the remaining sketches. The results are shown in Table 6.3.

The performance difference between SKS without pressure (SKS) and SKS with pressure (SKS-Press) is substantial; a more than 12 % reduction in EER. The performance improvement for the random forgery scenario is less significant than that of the skilled forgery scenario. This is reasonable because in the random forgery case, the shape and directional components of the sketch are already mostly distinct. Thus, there is not much to improve upon. However, for skilled forgeries the shape and direction components are as similar as humanly possible. Therefore, we can attribute the performances differences between SKS and SKS-Press to the biometric pressure. In every skilled forgery scenario tested: 3, 4, and 5 example sketches, the best performance is achieved by the addition of pressure.

Table 6.3 Performance comparison between the sketch-based password system with and without biometric pressure. Observe how the pressure makes an improvement in performance in almost all cases: all skilled forgery scenarios, and the 5 example case for random forgeries

Method	# Examples	EER_{rd}	EER_{sk}
SKS	3	**2.5**	17.8
SKS-Press	3	3.5	**10.7**
SKS	4	**2.5**	16.6
SKS-Press	4	4.1	**3.7**
SKS	5	1.6	14.0
SKS-Press	5	**0.0**	**3.3**

6.3 Key Points

The major points from this chapter include:

1. Experimental results support the fact that the SKS model is locally unique and tolerant.
2. Performance analysis demonstrates that SKS is comparable to DTW *without* biometrics.
3. The addition of pressure significantly improves performance.

References

1. M. Martinez-Diaz, J. Fierrez, C. Martin-Diaz, and J. Ortega-Garcia. DooDB: A Graphical Password Database Containing Doodles and Pseudo-Signatures. *12th Int'l. Conf. on Frontiers in Handwriting Recognition*, pages 339–344, 2010.
2. M. Martinez-Diaz, J. Fierrez, and J. Galbally. The DooDB Graphical Password Database: Data Analysis and Benchmark Results. *IEEE Access*, 1:596–605, 2013.
3. B. S. Riggan, W. E. Snyder, X. Wang, and J. Feng. A human factors study of graphical passwords using biometrics. *Proc. of the 36th German Conf. on Pattern Recognition*, 2014.

Chapter 7
Conclusions

Abstract The concluding chapter of this brief summarizes the fundamental concepts of sketch-based password discussed in this work. First, a general overview of this brief, which broadly highlights the relevant literature associated with graphical authentication systems and biometrics and emphasizes similarities and differences between DTW and SKS. Then, the major contributions of this brief, which include the new qualitative and quantitative analysis, are restated. The primary implication from the contributions of this brief is that a generalized SKS framework improves both the security and usability of a sketch-based authentication system, especially one that utilizes biometric information. Beyond the specific implementations in this brief, similar types of analyses may prove beneficial in future extensions and other applications. Lastly, the major experimental results are provided, which include 12 % reduction in equal error rate (EER) when adding pressure as biometric features and the 17 % reduction in EER on the BioSketch database.

Keywords DTW · SKS · Sketch-based password · Similarity measures · Security · Usability

In this brief, the fundamentals of sketch-based authentication systems were introduced. The overview of existing graphical password and biometric systems provides the necessary basis for better understanding sketch-based recognition. The primary methods for recognizing sketch-based passwords that are discussed include: DTW and SKS. These methods both focus on measuring the dissimilarity/similarity between to sketch-based passwords, however, each achieves this using differing assumptions. The primary differences between these two methods include: (1) parameterization, (2) operating space, and (3) computational complexity. Additionally, two methods for comparing a sketch with multiple exemplars are considered for both DTW and SKS. Therefore, the basics for constructing a sufficiently discriminative sketch-based authentication system are provided.

The novel contributions of this brief included the theoretical analysis of SKS and experimental comparisons with DTW and the Fréchet distance. The theoretical analysis showed that SKS is an efficient, secure, and robust discriminative approach for recognizing sketch-based passwords. The experimental results demonstrate that SKS is comparable to DTW *without the inclusion of biometric pressure*, and the SKS similarity semi-metric is better suited for sketch-based authentication systems than the Fréchet distance metric. Also, the variability analysis provided demonstrates that SKS is sufficiently capable of distinguishing both random forgeries and skilled forgeries from genuine sketch-based passwords. Unlike the Fréchet distance, SKS was shown to capture an intuitive measure of similarity by having a more restricted definition of "different."

The results provided show the potential application of SKS to sketch-based authentication. The experimental results demonstrated that as features were added to SKS, no detrimental effects due to the *curse of dimensionality* were observed. In general, the experimental results showed that DTW and SKS achieve similar performances, *without* biometrics. However, SKS is more general than DTW. The additional restrictions, such as boundary conditions and monotonic constraints, that DTW impose on the optimization problem makes DTW less robust. SKS, which does not impose such constraints, is free to accumulate evidence of similarity between a sketch and a model. The addition of pressure as a biometric features was shown to increase the level of performance by more than 12 %. When comparing SKS and Fréchet distance, the HCI study showed that the confusion between genuine sketch-based passwords and forgeries was less for SKS. Plus, SKS was shown to reduced the skilled EER by more than 17 % using the BioSketch database.

7.1 Future Work

While the results are promising, more work is necessary in order to determine the true level of security for sketch-based passwords. There are many possible extensions to the studies provided in this brief, such as comparing different modes of biometrics (e.g. fingerprints, faces, and sketch-based passwords with biometric properties). More directly, SKS may be further improved by estimating local smoothing parameters or using subspace approximations. Lastly, other applications may exist in higher spatial dimensions (e.g. gesture recognition using range cameras). The authors hope to study some of the extensions in future research.

Appendix A Optimization

In Chap. 3, the representative model was constructed by simply averaging the models. The average is optimal if the models being averaged are sufficiently close in the space of models and the space is approximately Euclidean. However, because the space is very high dimensional there are no guarantees, especially due to noise, high intra-class variation, and discontinuities. Therefore, it may be useful to define an optimization problem.

Optimization is defined as "the science of determining the 'best' solutions to certain mathematically defined problems" [2]. In this chapter, the problem of constructing a representative model is posed as an optimization problem. Here, two approaches are suggested:

1. optimizing the squared error
2. optimizing the geodesic distance

Note that an optimal model, according to the objective function, does not necessarily mean that recognition performance will improves. The objective function must accurately represent the problem. In many applications, the objective function being optimized is not the "real" problem, however, the "real" problem may be ill-posed and much too difficult to solve. Therefore, in some cases, a simpler objective function is constructed so that the solution may be well defined.

A.1 Squared Error

A common optimization problem involves minimizing the squared error, by some defined error term. This is widely used in neural network applications [3]. The error in this application is considered the Euclidean distance between models. Directly, the optimization problem is stated as follows:

$$\underset{\varphi}{\text{minimize}} \sum_{i=1}^{n} \|\varphi - \varphi_i\|^2$$

where φ and φ_i are models.

© The Author(s) 2014
B. S. Riggan et al., *Fundamentals of Sketch-Based Passwords,*
SpringerBriefs in Computer Science, DOI 10.1007/978-3-319-13629-5

This, of course, yields

$$\varphi = \frac{1}{n} \sum_{i=1}^{n} n\varphi_i$$

which is the average model.

However, if we redefine the model as a function of the input sketch. This indirect optimization problem becomes:

$$\underset{\alpha}{\text{minimize}} \sum_{i=1}^{n} \|\varphi(\boldsymbol{\alpha}) - \varphi(\boldsymbol{\alpha}_i)\|^2$$

It can be shown that the solution to this problem has the form

$$\sum_{i=1}^{n} (\varphi(\boldsymbol{\alpha}) - \varphi(\boldsymbol{\alpha}_i)) \frac{\partial \varphi}{\partial \boldsymbol{\alpha}} = 0.$$

Note the differences in these two optimization problems. The first seek to find the model φ that minimizes the squared error (in this case Euclidean distance) between each model, and as shown, the answer is the average model. The second problem seeks to find the sketch $\boldsymbol{\alpha}$ that minimizes the squared error between each model. Although, they are similar problems (and should result in a similar solution), the second problem relates the optimization back to the input sketch.

A.2 Geodesic

Similarly, if one considers to account for the nonlinearity of the "space of models" a geodesic distance may be defined, and then this distance may used in the optimization problem. Before we constructing this type of optimization problem, let us first define the term geodesic.

A parameterized curve γ is called a *geodesic* if the tangent vector field is parallel along γ [1]. Equivalently, if $D_\gamma \gamma' = 0$ (i.e. the acceleration vector is normal to the surface), where $D_\gamma \gamma'$ represents the covariant derivative of the vector field γ' with respect to γ.

Now, consider the following optimization problem:

$$\underset{\alpha}{\text{minimize}} \sum_{i=1}^{n} \delta\left(\varphi(\boldsymbol{\alpha}), \varphi(\boldsymbol{\alpha}_i)\right)^2$$

where $\delta(\,\cdot\,)$ represents the geodesic distance between two models.

The solution takes the following form:

$$\sum_{i=1}^{n} \frac{\partial \delta}{\partial \varphi} \frac{\partial \varphi}{\partial \boldsymbol{\alpha}} = 0.$$

Note that derivatives may have to be approximated in order to obtain a solution.

References

1. R. L. Bishop and S. I. Goldberg. *Tensor analysis on manifolds*. Dover Publications, 1980.
2. R. Fletcher. *Practical Methods of Optimization*. John Wiley & Sons, 2nd edition, 1987.
3. S. Haykin. *Neural networks and learning machines*, chapter 4. Prentice Hall, 3rd edition, 2008.

Appendix B Subspace Approximations

There are many methods, including PCA, RPCA, and KPCA, that attempt to reduced the dimensionality of models or descriptors. The advantage reducing the number of dimensions is to alleviate the effects from the "curse of dimensionality" [1]. This also produces a subspace approximation in which many times the models become more representative of their class.

In this chapter, both PCA and KPCA are discussed specifically in the context of the sketch-based password system introduced in this dissertation.

B.1 PCA

Given a set of observed feature vectors, $\{\mathbf{v}_1, \mathbf{v}_2, \ldots, \mathbf{v}_n\}$, such that

$$\sum_{i=1}^{n} \mathbf{v}_i = 0,$$

PCA diagonalizes the covariance matrix:

$$C = \frac{1}{n} \sum_{i=1}^{n} \mathbf{v}_i \mathbf{v}_i^T. \tag{B.1}$$

This decomposition is performed by solving the following eigenvalue problem

$$\lambda \mathbf{e} = C \mathbf{e}. \tag{B.2}$$

Let the set of eigenvectors $\left\{\mathbf{e}_1^*, \mathbf{e}_2^*, \ldots, \mathbf{e}_d^*\right\}$, which span the d-dimensional space, be the solution to the eigenvalue problem corresponding non-negative eigenvalues $\left\{\lambda_1^*, \lambda_2^*, \ldots, \lambda_d^*\right\}$ in descending order. Then, the principle components are consider to be the eigenvectors corresponding to the k largest eigenvalues, where $k < d$. These k principle components may be used to form a linear subspace, which is useful for reducing the dimensionality of the features $\mathbf{v}_i$ for $i = 1 \ldots n$.

© The Author(s) 2014
B. S. Riggan et al., *Fundamentals of Sketch-Based Passwords*,
SpringerBriefs in Computer Science, DOI 10.1007/978-3-319-13629-5

Assuming the features $\mathbf{v}_i$ lie in d-dimensional space, each point may be projected into the linear subspace formed by the principle eigenvectors. That is,

$$
\tilde{\mathbf{v}}_i = \begin{bmatrix} \underline{\quad} & \mathbf{e}_1^* & \underline{\quad} \\ \underline{\quad} & \mathbf{e}_2^* & \underline{\quad} \\ & \vdots & \\ \underline{\quad} & \mathbf{e}_k^* & \underline{\quad} \end{bmatrix} \mathbf{v}_i
$$

for $i = 1...n$.

In regard to this brief, a model may be constructed from these projected features (with reduced number of dimensions). Therefore, the model equation becomes the following:

$$
m(\tilde{\mathbf{v}}) = \frac{1}{z} \sum_{i=1}^{n} \exp\left(-\frac{1}{2}(\tilde{\mathbf{v}} - \tilde{\mathbf{v}}_i)^T \boldsymbol{\Sigma}^{-1}(\tilde{\mathbf{v}} - \tilde{\mathbf{v}}_i) \right). \tag{B.3}
$$

Since dimensionality of the feature vectors effect the size of the model, reducing the dimensionality of the feature vectors makes computing the model more efficient. The danger in reducing the dimensionality too much is that the models from two distinct classes (i.e. different passwords) may be confused with one another.

B.2   KPCA

In the previous section, a subspace approximation of the model was constructed using PCA. Here, the subspace is constructed using nonlinear principle components, but the approach is very similar.

Consider a nonlinear mapping, $\Phi : \mathbb{R}^d \to \mathcal{G}$, where $\mathcal{G}$ denotes the feature space of arbitrary size. Similar to before, the observed features are assumed to be centered (this time in the feature space), meaning

$$
\sum_{i=1}^{n} \Phi(\mathbf{v}_i) = 0.
$$

Now, consider performing PCA (as discussed previously) in the feature space $\mathcal{G}$. Therefore, the covariance matrix

$$
C' = \frac{1}{n} \sum_{i=1}^{n} \Phi(\mathbf{v}_i)\Phi(\mathbf{v}_i)^T
$$

is diagonalized by solving the following eigenvalue problem:

$$
\lambda \mathbf{E} = C' \mathbf{E} \tag{B.4}
$$

This time the eigenvectors, $\{\mathbf{E}_1^*, \mathbf{E}_2^*, \ldots, \mathbf{E}_d^*\}$, lie in $\mathcal{G}$ instead of $\mathbb{R}^d$. Therefore, when the eigenvectors are projected back into the original space, they are nonlinear. Using the k principal eigenvectors, a similar approach may be used to project the feature vectors into the nonlinear subspace constructed using KPCA and then construct a model.

There are, however, some considerations when using KPCA. One consideration is the fact that the mapping, Φ, is unknown. Therefore, the eigenvalue problem is solved using kernel methods; hence, "kernel" PCA. Another consideration is the centering the data in the input space does not guarantee that the projected data is also centered. Therefore, a slight modification must be made (see [2]).

References

1. R. Bellman. *Dynamic Programming*. Princton University Press, 1957.
2. B. Schölkopf, A. Smola, and K. Muller. Nonlinear component analysis as a kernel eigenvalue problem. *Neural Computation*, 10(5):1299–1319, 1998.